MANCHESTER
AT WAR
1939–45
THE PEOPLE'S STORY

MANCHESTER
AT WAR
1939–45
THE PEOPLE'S STORY

Graham Phythian

This book is dedicated to the memory
of my mother and father …
promises fulfilled.

First published 2014

The History Press
The Mill, Brimscombe Port
Stroud, Gloucestershire, GL5 2QG
www.thehistorypress.co.uk

© Graham Phythian, 2014

The right of Graham Phythian to be identified as the Author
of this work has been asserted in accordance with the
Copyright, Designs and Patents Act 1988.

British Library Cataloguing in Publication Data.
A catalogue record for this book is available from the British Library.

ISBN 978 0 7524 9102 8

Typesetting and origination by The History Press
Printed in Great Britain

CONTENTS

Instinctively, one recognised the calibre of these people. An intense sense of unity has been created.

If Hitler visualised these folk as shrieking and tearing their hair and cowering before his rage he had another guess coming.

When I penetrated to where the rivers of water ran through shattered glass and snuffed the tang of smoke and saw little flames flicker onto the skeletons of buildings … and grimy and weary firemen and ruddy-cheeked soldiers with fixed bayonets … I knew that I loved Manchester. Its dear smoky streets, its kindly, comradely folk, the very nooks and alleys of it – I loved it.

If this be the battle of Manchester then Hitler has lost it.

Manchester City News, *28 December 1940*

I see the damage done by the enemy attacks; but I also see, side by side with the devastation and amid the ruins, quiet, confident, bright and smiling eyes, beaming with a consciousness of being associated with a cause far higher and wider than any human or personal issue. I see the spirit of an unconquerable people.

Winston Churchill, April 1941

ACKNOWLEDGEMENTS

With thanks to: Andrew Schofield of the North West Sound Archive; Arthur Davenport, Dennis Wood and Duncan Broady of the Greater Manchester Police Museum and Archives; Peter Turner for access to Salford Oral Heritage Archives; Prestwich and Whitefield Heritage Society; Jill Cronin for liaison with Denton Local History Society; Helen Hibberd and Bernard Leach for liaison with Chorlton Good Neighbours; Duncan O'Reilly for loan of extracts from his mother's autobiography (Jeanne Herring); Philip Lloyd for loan of extracts from his mother's wartime diary (Mary Lloyd); James Gilmour for hospitality, access to his personal museum and archive, and liaison; Bob Potts, Diana Leitch and Greg Forster for liaison; Bernard Leach for permission to use extracts from his interview with Mickie Mitchell; Phil Blinston for art work and liaison; Bryant Anthony Hill, Dave Kierman, Bob Potts, Walter Jackson and Norman Williamson for loan of publications; the *Manchester Evening News*; the staff of Manchester Central Library Local Studies, the Imperial War Museum North, Stockport Air Raid Shelters Museum, Stockport Heritage and Archives, Salford Local Studies Library Museum and Archives, Prestwich Library, Tameside Local History Library, and Trafford Local Studies Library.

PREFACE

It was during the Second World War, for the first significant time in history, that the civilian populace was regarded as fair game as a military target. Post-Battle of Britain, it was Hitler's policy to carry out aerial attacks on British cultural and industrial centres, with destruction of nearby residential areas and the killing of non-military men, women and children regarded as justifiable collateral damage.

This book is a collection of memories of those brave and fortunate survivors of the Home Front in Manchester. But it is not just about the Blitz: naturally I include the testimony of those many Mancunians who exemplified the everyday courage of the 'Keep Calm and Carry On' variety. Dealing with the less immediately violent disruptions of evacuation, sundered families, rationing and the constant underlying fear of not knowing whether one's person, family, workplace or home would survive the next twenty-four hours, deserves commemorating just as much as front-line heroism. 'We just got on with the job' is a frequently recurring theme in these pages.

The story goes that Hitler's plans for Manchester included his personal use of the Midland Hotel on Peter Street, as it reminded him of a medieval castle. This is allegedly why the hotel and nearby streets remained untouched by bombs throughout the war. (Apparently any Luftwaffe pilot careless enough to allow the Midland to be hit would have had to attend a private audience with the Führer. One can imagine that this would not have consisted of a cosy chat over *Kaffee und Kuchen*.) Local tradition has it that Hitler, who by all accounts fancied himself as an architecture buff, had his eye on Rochdale Town Hall too, for similar reasons.

As the reader will soon discover, the definition of 'Manchester' in this book is elastic, stretching to cover the area roughly corresponding to the conurbation once known in council chambers as Greater Manchester County. The stories presented here, besides naturally having relevance to the city itself, not only stray into neighbouring Metropolitan boroughs, but also raise the local flag a few miles

Firemen at work in Portland Street during the Christmas Blitz 1940. (Manchester Evening News)

into south Lancashire and north Cheshire. It was, after all, one huge Luftwaffe target, for which I use 'Manchester' as a shorthand term.

So apologies to non-Mancunians, but a title such as 'Stretford, Chadderton, Flixton, Rochdale, Sale, Denton, Stockport, Salford, Ramsbottom, Urmston, Marple, Worsley, Prestwich, Audenshaw and Manchester at War' would not have made it past the editor.

I am also using this preface to justify the inclusion of an abridged version of my late father's account of his escape from a POW camp in Poland, and his journey across occupied Europe back home to Hulme, Manchester. This seems to be loosening the geographical boundaries to an unreasonable degree, but I have included the story not purely out of nepotism, but because firstly it's a grand yarn in itself, and secondly it's about how a Mancunian showed wartime qualities of ingenuity, courage and dogged persistence in another context. Besides, my father does not have the 'Coming Home' chapter all to himself.

I wish to thank all the contributors and their families who welcomed me into their home to conduct the taped interviews. The compilation of this book has been a fascinating learning experience for me, and in several instances, deeply moving. The full list of individual contributors is given at the end of the book.

My text sources were:

1. Transcripts of tape-recorded interviews made by me
2. Transcripts of recordings from the North West Sound Archive, Clitheroe
3. Written diaries and memoirs, used by permission
4. *Manchester Evening News* articles, cartoons, correspondence and adverts from 1939, 1941–42, 1945, 1989, and 2010

5. *Manchester Evening Chronicle* correspondence and articles from 1940 and 1945
6. *Manchester City News* items from 1940–45
7. Oral history passages, used by permission, from other books on the topic, a list of which is given in the bibliography at the end of the book
8. Extracts from two booklets published by the North West Sound Archive: Recollections: Heaton Park and Ramsbottom. 'Anon.' usually indicates a passage taken from one of these publications, in which names of contributors, although given in a generic list, are not attached to specific portions of text.

I have changed nothing from the original wording of the transcripts or text, except for the very occasional deletion of a repetition, or an even more occasional (and slight) rearranging of the order of words for clarity's sake. Items in square brackets that were not in the original transcript or text are my additions, and render the odd explanation, modern reference, or precise location of a detail supplied by the contributor.

Every reasonable effort has been made to trace the copyright owners of material, both textual and visual, used herein. Notice of any omissions or oversights should be sent in writing to the author, c/o The History Press.

Graham Phythian, 2014

ONE

EVACUEES' STORIES

The government had been planning the evacuation of children and some adults from major cities from August 1939. Two days before war was declared on 3 September, a total of 172,000 children and 23,000 adults were moved from Manchester into mostly private accommodation in the surrounding countryside. The evacuation took three days.

IVY CORRIGAN

When the war started we were evacuated to Poulton-le-Fylde, near Blackpool. I went to a school that was just a girls' school, St Simon's School. They were supposed to be just going to try it out for the weekend, and we went on the Friday and all the children were at the station. We had a pillowcase with just bits and pieces in that would last over the weekend, clothes for the weekend, all had a label on us with our names and addresses of the schools we came from, and piled into trains, and couldn't understand why all our mothers and fathers that were there at the station were weeping and looking really upset if it was only for the weekend. It was a bit of an adventure. I was nine then. And then during that weekend war was declared and so we were stuck there.

Going on the train was quite an adventure, but then when we got there we were taken to a school, and we were all sort of huddled around in the school hall and in the playground there, and people were coming up and saying, 'I'll have one boy,' or 'I'll have one girl,' or 'I'll take two children.' And that was a bit soul-destroying, really, because you had to stand there looking as if you were selling yourself! That was a bit hard.

(Courtesy of Life Times Oral History Collection, Salford Museum and Art Gallery)

ARTHUR ROBERT DAVENPORT

My parents decided when it was time for me to attend school in September 1939 I would be evacuated to Rose Hill, Marple, to live with an honorary uncle and aunt, Harold and Margaret Miller, with their two daughters at No. 1 Weatherley Drive. My parents and I travelled by bus from Culcheth Lane [Newton Heath] to London Road railway station [now Piccadilly station] and caught a steam engine – always a thrill – to Rose Hill station. Rose Hill in those days was mostly countryside with rabbits running in the fields. There were lots of wildlife, different trees and fields with long hedgerows. There was even a blacksmith on the road from Rose Hill to Marple. A great change from sooty Newton Heath.

The school I attended in Rose Hill was a nearby private school. I only attended for the first term and then I returned home, as my parents thought as there had been very little to worry about it was fairly safe, and if the worst came to the worst – if we were going to die – we would all die together.

JEANNE HERRING

In line with many other schools, Whalley Range evacuated its pupils. We went to Stacksteads, near Bacup in the Rossendale Valley. My sister Sylvia was on holiday with her aunt in Nottingham when war was declared, so she stayed there as she was fourteen and able to leave school. People were called up to do war work and Sylvia worked in a munitions factory during the war.

I can remember elder sister Kathleen coming to the house the morning I left for (at that time) an unknown destination. She had bought me a black patent leather case for my gas mask and a silver identity bracelet. Mother asked why I needed a bracelet and I said, 'it is in case I get bombed or burned, you will recognise my body.' Mother burst into tears and I got a strong ticking off from Kathleen.

I don't remember much about leaving Manchester. I think it was from Chorlton station, but I do recall arriving in Bacup with my suitcase, gas mask in its posh case and a leather school satchel on my back. We were taken to a church hall and divided into groups, each of us having a label tied to a coat button. We were issued with a brown carrier bag containing a tin of corned beef, a tin of sardines and a tin of fruit with evaporated milk. The word 'evaporated' always intrigued me, for it wasn't evaporated.

A woman in WRVS uniform, armed with a clipboard, marched us up a narrow street of terraced houses, dropping off pupils on the way. I was the only one left and could see no more houses, but further up the lane we came to a small farmhouse with an elderly couple waiting at the front door. Their names were Polly and Johnny Lord, and I was to spend the next four months with them.

Evacuees boarding the train at the old Chorlton-cum-Hardy station, the day before the declaration of war on 3 September 1939. The train's destination was the Derbyshire Peak District. *(Manchester Central Library Local Images Collection: M09913)*

I really missed my family, but the couple were so good and kind to me that overall I quite enjoyed the experience.

It was only a small farm, with seven cows, a horse for pulling the milk float, hens in a shed behind the house, and a couple of fields. The government made a small contribution to Polly and Johnny for my upkeep.

The arrangement for our continued education was that we attended Bacup and Rawtenstall Grammar School in the mornings and their pupils went in the afternoon. We didn't see much of them and I was never aware of any trouble between the two schools. Any we did meet were friendly and curious and a little bit sorry for us because we had had to leave our homes.

I enjoyed helping Polly around the house, collecting eggs and occasionally going round with Johnny on the cart delivering milk to the nearby houses. I used to balance the churn on my knee and tip the milk into a ladle and then into the customer's jug.

Polly rooted out a pair of clogs for me to wear in the shippen [cattle shed]. She told me that they had belonged to her daughter who had died of meningitis when she was thirteen. I asked her whether my arrival had brought back sad memories but she said, 'Memories, but not sad, it's lovely having you.' I felt very privileged. Talking of the cowshed, I did try my hand at milking, but with little success.

The couple had occasional help from John, a farm labourer who invited friends, teachers and me to a moonlight walk on the moors. I remember it well. The clear sky, the silvery look of the streams running down the hillside and the boggy moss and grass underfoot – all quite exciting for us city folk.

Another time I went with Johnny to fetch the horse from the field and was invited to sit on her back for the journey home. I'd never sat on a horse before and imagined a gentle trot, but Johnny slapped the horse's rump and shouted, 'Home, lass.' The horse shot forward with me clinging to her mane, shaking with fright. It was probably only half a mile to the farm but it felt like forever.

The food on the farm was good; plenty of dairy products, chicken and good casserole stews cooked in the oven on the open kitchen range, better in fact than rations in Manchester.

NORMAN WILLIAMSON

I went to Central High School in town, and we were evacuated to Blackpool. Most of the boys went into boarding houses in big batches, ten or twenty, but I was picked out by a family that lived inland, maybe two miles inland. They were very nice people, but I couldn't really settle there. She had a son, he wasn't doing very well at school and I think they wanted me to try and help him out, and I did. I used to do his homework for him, but he was finally caught out when he went to school and he was the only one in the class that got his homework right. So he was supposed to go out and show them how he did it, but he couldn't! He was a bit of a spoilt brat, really.

So I thought, I'll make my escape! They were watching the bus station and the railway station, but I thought, I'll make my escape, go back home and get a job, as I was fourteen. I'll mingle in with the crowds at the bus station or the railway station, and get on a bus or train unnoticed. I got my plans all drawn up, however, just as my well-laid escape plans were about to be put into action, my mother turned up! I said, 'I can't stay here, I'm coming home.' Anyway, we had a long talk, and I said, 'I don't care, I'm not staying!' So she had a word with this lady, and she brought me home.

If I'd been with the lads on the coast, I'd have been happier. I remember a ship had been sunk out at sea, and there were oranges all over the beach! [laughs]

I did go down to see them. I remember the RAF bombers sort of skimming over the piers, very low.

HELEN SEPHTON

I was an early evacuee, because I was only one year of age when the war started. I think it was a matter of seeing as how a bomb hit the next street where we were on – Abbey Hey Lane [Gorton] – and flattened it. I think my parents then realised it was a matter of urgency to get the children all out of the way. My father then – he didn't have to do – but he joined the Royal Marines, the submarines, and my mother was away nursing people at Crumpsall Hospital. So they both had these respective careers.

My brothers had been sent to a farm in Norfolk, but they wanted a different place for me. I don't know how they came across these people's name, address [a farm in Glossop] or what-have-you, but they were called Flaherty. I never knew her first name, but I called him 'Uncle Jimmy', and I must have gone to them when I was around two, just a tot, and I think I was about three years with them.

I remember snippets of it, you know, things jump out at me, but I was only young. 'Auntie Flaherty' as I called her, she was the stern one, she was the disciplinarian. I could twist Uncle Jimmy round my finger. I remember sitting on a pig and thinking I could go cowboy style, you know, round the farm, which didn't work out as I remember falling off, and I remember the chastisement I got off Auntie Flaherty [laughs] as a result of it. I remember sitting with little fluffy chickens on my shoulders and jumping when I saw her appear you know, [laughs] a couple of them fell off, I was absolutely mortified when these little chickens fell to the floor.

The kitchen had a long sink made of stone, and just the one tap, which was cold. My job was, I wiped the eggs clean, and I can't remember ever dropping one. I think I would have remembered that! I love eggs to this day, but I swear I had egg for breakfast, dinner and tea when I was on the farm, all done in different ways.

I had a free run of the farm. I don't know how I didn't get into serious trouble, because farms are a dangerous place. I remember seeing Uncle Jimmy in the field, you know, on a tractor, and not realising at that time that tractors have a blind spot; the driver can't see little things below in front of them because of these big wheels and things going round. I remember running in front, running up to the tractor and shouting, 'Uncle Jimmy! Uncle Jimmy!' but of course he couldn't hear me because of the sound of the tractor, and he couldn't see me, because I was only a tot, and he was coming straight towards me. And I don't know how I got out of the way, I really don't, but well I must have done. And I was horrified, I thought, 'Why is he coming towards me and not turning round?' I was probably about four, something like that.

EVELYN SEYMOUR

I was brought up in Salford. I was evacuated to Accrington when I was six years old, and because I was so young my sister came with me. She should have gone to Lancaster, but stayed with this lady in Accrington. She looked after us very well: I had my seventh birthday there, and she let me have half a dozen children from school, and we nearly wrecked the place! But she was quite happy, she loved children.

I only stayed in Accrington from the September until the Christmas, 1939. My mother used to come up every weekend to see us, and she found out it was too expensive. She decided she just couldn't afford it, and wages were not very high in those days. My father was working, but with three children, we found it very difficult.

MARGARET GREAVES

I was fourteen – well, fourteen-and-a-half really – as the war broke out in the September. I went to Fallowfield Technical High School for Girls, having passed my eleven plus, and I was evacuated to Macclesfield. The week before, I'd been on holiday at my aunt's in Kendal, and she said, 'Let's go to Morecambe for the day.' So my cousin and I went to Morecambe. And then my mother suddenly appeared from Manchester, she said, 'You've got to come home! You've got to be evacuated.' That was the Thursday or Friday before September 3rd, then I was evacuated to Macclesfield with the school. I was billeted in Broken Cross with a very nice family with two little girls; he was the manager of one of the silk mills.

We had part-time education: one week we'd go in mornings, and the next week we'd go in afternoons. And this continued from the September to the December, and nothing happened. There was no war, I mean, it was just like being on holiday in a way, part-time school, you know, which I didn't enjoy very much.

I was a singer, I've always been a singer, and the Christmas of that year, 1939, we had a carol service in Macclesfield Parish Church, and I was singing two solos out of the Messiah. There's a story attached to that, because when a lady who was in the congregation and who belonged to our church – don't ask me why she was in Macclesfield at that time, I've no idea – she came back and said, 'How is it that Margaret Lord' – my maiden name was Lord – 'can sing in Macclesfield, and she can't sing in our church?' Ladies were not considered to be part of the choir, you see, they used to sit at the back of the choir stalls. But then, of course, the ladies were much in demand, because the young men were at war.

So my parents said that as nothing had happened, I came home for Christmas, and then went back to Macclesfield. The girl I was billeted with was called Audrey Long, she was a very tall girl, and she was good at long jumping [laughs], I can remember, and I often wonder what's happened to her, because I've had no contact with her. The lady became ill, and we both had to separate then, and I was put with a young couple who had no idea how to cope with a teenager – by this time I was nearly fifteen – I wouldn't say I was unhappy, but I was uncomfortable. This was still in Broken Cross. Anyway my parents decided that nothing had happened, so I could go back home.

RUTH PALMER

I was only six when they gave me a gas mask, put a label round my neck like Paddington Bear and took me to a big posh house in Chapel-en-le-Frith, Derbyshire. And I hated it.

They had a nanny for their little girl, and a rose garden and a swing, which I thought was very posh. They also had a breakfast room and I couldn't imagine anyone having a special room just to have their breakfast in.

The nanny used to scrub and scrub my back in the bath every night. It was all very different and I wanted my Mam, and when she came for me I was glad and I think the posh family were too. My mother was staying in an ordinary house at the other end of the village with my younger sister and the three of us all slept in one bed and I was happy again.

(Manchester Evening News supplement, 5 September 1989)

HILDA MASON

My two brothers were evacuated, to Knutsford, where they lived with a family. I wasn't, because I'd just started work. They got on very well with the family, because the family they stayed with was connected with Tatton Park. He used to be a gamekeeper there, and he used to take my brothers round the Park. We used to go and visit them at weekends, and we used to play on the heath – football – with them, and they were there a couple of years.

ROSA SLATER

Well, I was evacuated first with the school to a place called Wilpshire [north of Blackburn], with a 'P' in the middle. I don't know where it is, somewhere up north, and we were in a schoolroom and people picked you and took you.

I got picked by this lady and she had quite a posh house, and she put me in the attic on a camp bed – which I didn't mind, you know, and then she told me to come downstairs and she told me I would not be eating with her daughter or her, I would be eating in the back room with the maidservant or whoever it was, you know, and then I would have certain chores to do before I went to school and certain chores to do when I came back. One of them was black-lead this grate in this pantry affair, which took me all of three or four nights. I mean, I was big and boisterous you know, I had plenty of energy then, but I mean it was such a huge thing – it was ridiculous. And then the food was dreadful.

Leaflet outlining the

Arrangements for Evacuation from Manchester

(except Wythenshawe)

in the event of an

Emergency

Reason for the Leaflet

Everyone hopes that Evacuation will never be necessary, but it is important to be prepared. You may already be familiar with the Government Scheme as a result of information given on the Wireless, in the Press, by Head Teachers, at Parents' Meetings, and in other ways. But it has been thought that it may be helpful to you to have a brief outline of the plans that have been made for Manchester, excepting Wythenshawe.

Persons for whom Evacuation Plans have been made

Evacuation has been arranged for :—

(1) School children in school parties in charge of their teachers ;

(2) Children under five with their mothers or with some suitable woman chosen by the parents to go and remain with them ;

(3) Women expecting childbirth ;

(4) Blind Men and Women ;

(5) Cripples able to travel.

Those suffering, or suspected to be suffering, from infectious disease, cannot be evacuated until recovery.

It is voluntary : only those will be taken who wish to go. They will be conveyed by train (and in very special cases by road) to places in Lancashire, Derbyshire, Cheshire, Staffordshire, or Shropshire.

It is important to register, and this can be done at School or the nearest Maternity and Child Welfare Centre.

How we shall hear about Evacuation

If an emergency comes, there will be announcements on the Wireless and in the Newspapers : and these will tell you when evacuation will begin. On the first day most of the School Parties will leave, and on the second, and possibly other days, the remainder and the other classes.

Where to Assemble for Evacuation

Most parents have already made their arrangements with the Principal Teachers and those arrangements should be kept.

School Children

School children will assemble at the schools they attend, to go with their teachers.

But parents wanting to send all the children of the family together should send them to the same elementary school.

Mothers with Children under five years of age

Mothers going with their children under five years of age will assemble at the school from which their older children have gone on the previous day.

Mothers (or substitutes) without older children should go to the nearest elementary school. A mother having older children, as well as children under five, may take them with her instead of sending them with the school party. (N.B.— She should assemble at the school which one or more of these children attend.)

Mothers approaching childbirth have been notified of the assembly point by the Health Visitor, and they should go to it. Other mothers expecting childbirth should assemble at the nearest elementary school.

Blind and Cripples

Blind persons and adult cripples will follow the instructions already given them by the Home Visitor.

At each School or assembly point there will be teachers or other responsible persons who will direct the arrangements for evacuation.

Every person to be evacuated under the Scheme should make absolutely certain now as to the place of assembly for the day of evacuation.

ALL persons other than school children desiring evacuation must attend at their assembly point between 6 and 8 p.m. on the first Evacuation Day, to complete arrangements for their own evacuation.

Cost for Evacuation

There will be no charge for transport. Board and lodging will, in the first instance, be provided free for all children in school parties, but the Government may ask for a contribution from parents able to afford it. Lodging only will be provided for adults, and for the children who go with their mothers. Persons without means in the reception areas, who have been evacuated under the Scheme, should apply at the Ministry of Labour's office for allowances.

Clothing

In addition to the clothes which those to be evacuated are wearing, it is desirable that they should take with them, in a rucksack, haversack, or other suitable carrier, a complete change of underclothing, an overcoat or mackintosh, and also comb, towel, soap, face cloth, toothbrush, and an extra pair of boots or shoes. All must take their gas masks, which should be in boxes or carriers.

Food

Enough food for the day should be taken : but no bottles or liquids except for babies. Each person evacuated will be supplied with food at the end of the journey.

Identification

The name of the person evacuated should be written on the gas mask box or container : and he or she should carry a label giving name and home address and an identity disc which will be supplied at the School or Assembly Point. It would be well also to carry a stamped addressed postcard so that it may be posted home on arrival.

Further Information

Enquiries may be made of Head Teachers, Superintendents of Maternity and Child Welfare Centres, Health Visitors, and School Attendance Officers, or addressed to the Director of Education, Education Offices, Deansgate, Manchester, 3.

August, 1939.

Extracts from the evacuation leaflet disseminated in Manchester in the summer of 1939. *(Philip Lloyd)*

And then I wrote to my mum, I gave them to the lady to post and she never posted them. And my mother got worried because she never heard from me, and she wrote to the woman, who wrote back and said I'd not wrote. Something like that. Anyway, my mother came and got me. I told her I had written every week, twice a week, and I wasn't happy and that. So she told her what to do with her fancy house and whatever, so she brought me home.

I was home [in Cheetham Hill] for about a week I think, and then she took me to my auntie's in Newton in Montgomeryshire then, I think it's Powys now. I was there for about a year – I can't remember just how long – and I went to Penygloddfa Council School and it was lovely.

(North West Sound Archive)

ANON.

I went to St Joseph's School [Ramsbottom]. We had a class of pupils from one of the Manchester Catholic schools, St Bridgit's. We all tended to get on well together and mixed in, though they were kept in a class of their own. One of their teachers came with them and taught them all together. There was a spare classroom at St Joseph's and they used that.

(North West Sound Archive)

ROY MATHER

Where I lived was at Glossop, Derbyshire, and in the evacuation they brought schools from Higher Openshaw, round that area, West Gorton. The children came on the train with their labels and everything else, the gas mask box, and they had a sort of a rucksack thing. They got off the train at Glossop, which is only ten miles from Openshaw, and the local education people from the council took these children to where they'd had a response, where they'd said they'd take the children. The problem, what happened if there was a brother and sister, or two sisters, they separated them, and that didn't go down well.

Manchester Education Committee granted 1 shilling [5p] a head for Christmas treats to evacuated children. Number has dropped from 20,000 last Christmas to 5,000.

(Manchester City News, 14 December 1940)

What happened was, we went in our own classes, one week we went in a morning, the next week in the afternoon, and while we was in school they was out. And then eventually the phoney war was on, and they all filtered back home again, because there was nothing happening. It didn't happen until 1940, and this is 1939 we're talking about.

PHILIP LLOYD

Because my sister was under five years old, of course she wasn't going to school, so we were able to make our own arrangements and I was able to go along with my mother and younger sister. So we went to our grandmother's sister's in Wilmslow – Lacey Green – and I went to a little village school, a little stone-built school at the end of the road, for a term or two. It's been knocked down, and the Community Centre is there now.

Things were quiet in Manchester, so we came back here, and in fact we were here just in time for the Manchester Blitz! We were in our own shelter in the cellar, underneath the post office in Upper Chorlton Road. We'd had it strengthened, and my sister and I used to sleep down there during the worst of the Blitz. I can remember feeling the bombs dropping, the blast from them, I think one fell in the road just outside, and one of the shop windows was put through. It couldn't be replaced at the time, and had to be boarded up.

TWO

UNDER
ATTACK

Piccadilly warehouses ablaze during the December 1940 Blitz. The Fire Service was
temporarily understaffed, as many regular firemen had been called over to Liverpool to
combat the results of the bombing there. (Manchester Evening News)

*Although there were sporadic raids on Manchester and the surrounding area during
1940–41, the major bombardment was over the two nights of 22 and 23 December 1940:
the so-called 'Christmas Blitz'. The raw figures are enough to set the scene: over the two
nights a total of 467 tons of high explosive were dropped on the City of Manchester alone,
as well as around 2,000 canisters of incendiary bombs. Ten thousand incendiaries were
dropped on Salford. Nearly 800 people were killed in Manchester city centre and Salford.
Some of the buildings completely destroyed were Cheetham's Hospital, the Corn Exchange,
the Free Trade Hall, Smithfield Market, and St Anne's church.*

ERNEST RIGBY

It occurred only a few weeks ago – scene: a cosy inn on Manchester's outskirts.

Around a table sat a few friends and the writer. We were settling the war
between us, each having his own idea of how to do it – as armchair critics will –
when a report like 10,000 thunderbolts absolutely deafened us.

We thought that the building had been struck, but it was the next door premises,
which, when we came to look at them, were almost demolished. Fortunately for
us, at the inn the only damage was that all the windows were broken. Another
20 yards our way, well, we should not have done much similar visiting.

The joke was that an ARP man popped his head in and said, 'Close all those
windows.' We told him that we should have a job as there were no windows to close.

(Manchester Evening Chronicle, *11 November 1940*)

DENNIS WOOD

When the Blitz came, obviously the prime purpose was to bomb the city to
terrify the citizens. I know they had targets, Metro Vicks and all that, but really it
was to try and kill off our morale.

Every man was doing something. I can't remember if it was compulsory or
not, but there were men who worked in town, in offices and so on, nine to five,
and at five o'clock, two or three nights a week, they had to stay in the building as
fire-watchers. They were just as they were: no uniform, no unit.

During a raid they're on the roof, with a stirrup pump and buckets of water,
because what they dropped first were the incendiary bombs, magnesium. If one
hit something it would detonate, and if you didn't put it out the magnesium
would burn for about twenty minutes. Apart from being a signal for the next
wave of bombers, it might have gone through the roof with that force, and it's
lying in an office, and within twenty minutes it's an inferno.

The Manchester Royal Infirmary was partly destroyed by a time bomb, which exploded shortly after the main Blitz had finished. A landmine had previously been cleared from the site. (Manchester Evening News)

HUGH VARAH

[The speaker was an auxiliary fireman.]
A large bomb had dropped straight down the lift shaft [at the Manchester Royal Infirmary], bringing the lifts and cables crashing down and the stairs crashing down with them. There was just a deep and empty abyss with a tangle of cables all

the way down to the basement. There was no way either up or down and it was impossible to get a turntable ladder near the building. Before we had a chance to work anything out, there was a shout of 'Take cover! Bomb coming down!' Crouched down in the rubble, I looked up into the blackness of the sky and I could see nothing unusual. Then I noticed what appeared to be a dark tent-like canopy – a parachute. Then I saw that there were two of them, so close that they were touching one another. As they came lower, I could make out a long black oil drum suspended between them. It was the first view I ever had of a landmine.

A swirling gust of wind blew the parachutes sideways, wrapping them around a chimney stack. It was fortunate that they did because I'd left diving for cover a bit late. The landmine came to rest with a thump against the chimney where it hung swaying on its lines, making a grating noise as it scraped to and fro against the brickwork. I'd been told by a bomb disposal chap that these landmines had to roll over to set them off, so if the canopy held it would be safe, but there was no guarantee that the lines wouldn't tear under the strain. There was a sudden scurrying as everyone made frantic efforts to move away.

(*From* Forgotten Voices of the Blitz and the Battle for Britain)

DR R.A. CRANNA

In Manchester, I think it was in 1940, at Christmas time, there was a fantastic, horrible, bombing raid. We didn't get much of that in Bolton, but we could see and hear it. The next day there was no transport. I walked into Manchester, walked to the Infirmary, to see whether I could offer my services, and I remember this little old woman being brought in. She had been dug out of the rubble that afternoon, and all she could say was how sorry she was that she was in this dirty state and usually she was a clean woman, and was so upset that people were seeing her covered in dust.

(*North West Sound Archive*)

JEANNE HERRING

Sometimes the air-raid warning siren would go and then we sat in the brick shelter on Chorlton Green until the all-clear sounded. One time Father came to walk me home with the anti-aircraft guns from Longford Park firing away. Shrapnel was falling and Father told me to lie down on the pavement against the wall of the houses opposite Oswald Road School. I protested that it would dirty my coat, but Father pushed me down anyway. It was the nearest he ever got to getting cross with me. He lay down beside me, protecting me with his arms.

DENNIS HUMPHRIES

It was at that time – late in 1940 – that the air raids commenced, usually late in the evening, and I can always remember it going cold when I heard the first siren; it was almost dusk. We all ran home [to Glastonbury Road, Stretford], and got in the shelter. As I recall, everybody was given an Anderson shelter. It was corrugated, very good quality steel. But we and the family next door – whose name escapes me – we joined our shelter with theirs, to make one big one.

The first occasion I remember that was really serious was when one particular night – I think we were in the house at the time – the first thing we knew was that there was a massive explosion in a place called Naden's Farm fields, which was at the end of Old Hall Road [present day Lostock Park], and this apparently was a landmine. The reason we never heard anything was because it came down by parachute. The idea was to hit Trafford Park, which was full of factories like Metropolitan Vickers, which made tanks. Naden's Farm wasn't a million miles from Trafford Park, in a direct line probably 300 yards. It was very close.

Another landmine landed on Moss Road/Davyhulme Road corner, which was about 400 yards from Metropolitan Vickers main gate; another fell on the corner of Melville Road, which was again very close to Trafford Park,

Fire engine and staff at Park Road Fire Station, Stretford, which dealt with fires in Trafford Park and surrounding areas. The author's late mother Renee Phythian (née Smith) is seated second from the right. *(Author's collection)*

very close to the railway line too. Other bombs fell later – I can't remember the actual date – one bomb landed on Urmston Lane, about 400 yards from the Robin Hood hotel, a large bomb. Urmston Lane of course was very old property, three-storey, cellars, and this particular bomb demolished two big three-storey properties.

Another bomb landed during that particular time – probably late 1940, early 1941 – on the place we're sat in now, Stretford Library. It didn't destroy the library, but it was badly damaged. Another bomb landed on Victoria Park School, which again was not a million miles from Trafford Park. I believe there were quite a lot of people killed by this bomb that landed on the school, Victoria Park School, because there was a shelter in the yard, it was brick built, with a concrete roof. The shelter was just four walls, a roof and an entrance, nothing inside, you took your own seat and your own blanket, but I believe that they were killed there. And in Stretford Cemetery, backing on to the tramline, there's this memorial to the victims of that particular bombing. All the names of the people they found are on it except one, and they never knew who he was. But they thought possibly he was a sailor from a ship, probably a foreign sailor, because the docks were close, as was the Ship Canal.

In 1941 there was a massive bombing raid – sorry, a massive incendiary raid – and it *was* massive. My brother and I went out of the shelter and it was like Blackpool illuminations, lights and fires everywhere. They were aiming for Trafford Park, but a lot missed the target, a lot of them fell on the Lostock housing estate, where we lived. Stretford High School for Girls was completely demolished. I can remember the next day we found bombs that had not gone off; they were on the railway line embankment, embedded in the embankment. Probably still there today, some of them.

A house four doors from us was set alight, but quickly put out with the sand, etc., they had. Another house on Glastonbury Road belonged to a Mr and Mrs Hurst and their son Geoffrey, that was on fire and that was a serious fire. My brother helped the people to bring out their furniture and put it in the street. The house was gutted, three hours later.

Also in 1941, when the incendiaries came, one very serious fire in Trafford Park was at a place called Rosser's, a big wood-yard, which set alight and burned for days. The other place they were aiming for was a power station, the one at Barton Bridge, another one in Trafford Park. And Lancashire Dynamo and Crypto factory [situated just north of the junction of what is now Wharfside Way and Sir Matt Busby Way], which made electric motors, was a prime target for German bombers.

The morning after the incendiary raid my father was walking over Trafford Bridge to visit his mother who lived in Salford, and all the ships underneath, the barges, were all on fire, and the metal of the bridge was red hot.

HARRY ABRAHAM

The Sunday 22 December [1940] was a Sunday I'll always remember. That was when the Blitz really started ...

They dropped a bomb that we called a 'Molotov Chandelier', which was full of flares and bombs. The sky used to light up with the flares, then the bombs and the flares used to explode, showering the incendiaries all over the place ...

All along the Irwell the barges were cut from their moorings and were on fire. The warehouses along the canal were lit up and well ablaze, as well as the streets. It was really terrifying, and anyone who said he was not frightened was lying ...

After that came the heavy stuff: large bombs and landmines. Those landmines used to be bigger than telephone boxes and were dropped by parachute; some went off in the air and some landed unexploded. One landed on the croft on Trafford Road [Ordsall Park, Salford] and when the girls came into work at Howarth's the next day they had tassels of silk cut from the parachute ...

A lot of men lost their lives running towards the landmines. Because the mines were attached to parachutes they thought they were enemy parachutists. But of course they weren't, and landmines would explode, killing anyone within easy range.

(From Memories of the Salford Blitz, Christmas 1940*)*

ANNIE GIBB

We lived in a row of houses [Livingstone Street, Chorlton-on-Medlock, near St Mary's Hospital] and out of three houses there was four out of four [killed] in one house, my grandma in our house, and my mother and I were badly injured. And next door there was eight in the house, and four out of eight were lost. It was near the hospital, Manchester Royal, it was called High Street, and now it's called Hathersage Road.

We got a direct hit by a landmine. Somebody stood on my head, while we were buried. My grandmother was killed, but my mother could talk to me. She'd have been on her own if we'd been evacuated. I was nine, just on my ninth birthday. We were there three and a half hours about, buried. I remember trying to get out, but my mother said, 'Don't, you're hurting me.' I don't remember them getting me out, but I remember sat on the top, where they were bandaging me up, and that was about seven o'clock in the morning. Somebody came out of a house and gave me a little box of chocolates. I don't know who she was, I couldn't see her or anything.

My mother was cut in her neck, about seven stitches, cut on the top of her arm, her tendon was cut through, and she was in hospital from 23 December; she was in Christmas and New Year, and right through to Easter. They took her to the

September 1940: high-explosive bomb damage in Medlock Street, Hulme, outside Gee's, the draper's shop. The gas main was fractured. *(Greater Manchester Police Museum and Archives)*

emergency at Winwick [Warrington], where the soldiers were, and she was there while about Easter.

When I was taken out of the hole that they dug me out of, the bomb site, the rescue men carried me to the ambulance, and I said, 'I've hurt my leg,' and he said, 'Yes, you have, love, we know, love.' And they carried me by my arms, one on either side of me, so they kind of trailed me along, out of the bombing. When I went in the hospital, a lot of the soldiers came in, and that was what's now Wythenshawe, Baguley Sanatorium, Baguley.

I was in hospital March, it could have been February, to August. You couldn't have visitors because it was still part of the sanatorium – once a fortnight you got them, and the soldiers couldn't talk to any of the patients, they wouldn't let them. They were worried I might lose my leg, but they gave me skin grafts, Professor Bentley the doctor's name was, and it must have been about six months, they let me go home.

And now when I get a bit, in a situation, I think, well I got out of my hole, and you know, my bricks and mortar [laughs], and seventy-two years later, I'm still here!

If you go to the Police Museum, some policemen there took pictures of all the bombing before it got really bad, but whether they're still there, whether they have exhibitions, I don't know.

But Piccadilly, you couldn't tell what was burning and what wasn't, it was terrible. My dad was a fireman, and there was like a lot of big warehouses there then, really posh-type warehouses, where the hotel is now.

ROY MATHER

My aunt had a newsagent's shop on York Street, in Hulme, and they dropped a bomb outside the shop; it was a newsagent's and tobacconist's. It wasn't a direct hit on the shop, but they dropped it and it fell in the middle of the road. It was before the Blitz [probably September 1940].

In Longsight, where I lived, they were looking for the railway yard on the Manchester-London line. They didn't drop any bombs there, but they dropped some on Ardwick Green, round there [less than a mile to the west]. That was in 1941, after the Blitz.

In '41 they dropped a bomb on Hyde Road, and it demolished the Picturedrome that stood next to the Apollo, and they hit part of the barracks, where the Manchester Artillery was garrisoned. And at the other end of Ardwick Green there was the army depot, which is still there to this day.

On the Blitz, the sirens went at 6.42 [that evening], and the all-clear went at 6.30 the next morning, so we had twelve hours of it. We all dived in the cellars, of course, wondering when the all-clear was going to go, but nothing happened because it was the next day. They hadn't built the bomb shelters on the street, not until after the Blitz – wiser after the event! They were built with brick, and concrete on the roof. They were on the street, on the surface.

The Artillery Barracks on Hyde Road, Ardwick, after the March 1941 bombing.
(Greater Manchester Police Museum and Archives)

When the fires got going, you could read a paper in the street by the glare from the fires in Manchester. We were only a mile and a half from the city. And then the guns were going off, and there was shrapnel from the guns, and after, we went looking for it in the street, and collecting it. It was very sharp, you know.

MARJORIE AINSWORTH

I was living in Gorton at the time, and my boyfriend, who I later married, lived in Bradford, Manchester. I remember that we had some sporadic air raids from about August 1940, and then the big Blitz was on 22 and 23 December of the same year. One memory of that is when my husband and I were at a party in Reddish on Christmas Eve, and the fires had been put out by then, but they'd had so many fire engines and fire services called from all the north-west to help. On Reddish Lane a fire engine came down and asked my husband if he knew the way to … somewhere, I've forgotten where, and he said, 'Well I couldn't tell you from here, but if you give us a lift, [laughs] I can put you on the right road!' So we had a lift on a fire engine up Reddish Lane and down Hyde Road, on the right road to get home.

Another vivid memory: Sunday cinemas weren't allowed then, but cinemas and theatres were allowed to have sort of special concerts. My husband and I went to Ardwick Hippodrome, and 'Hutch' – Leslie Hutchinson – was there. He was all the rage in the 1930s. He was a black man, a great ladies' man, and he played the piano in immaculate evening dress, and one of his gimmicks was a handkerchief with which he mopped his brow. During his performance the sirens went, and the manager came onto the stage and said, 'The sirens have gone. Do you want to all go home, or do you want him to carry on?' So we all shouted, 'Carry on!' So he was really mopping his brow! [laughs] It wasn't for show, any of that!

We could hear what was going on outside, but when we did finish up, we were walking down Hyde Road – we knew we'd have to walk home – and there were incendiary bombs lighting the pavements up, so were picking our way past these incendiary bombs, and we got as far as Hyde Road tram depot, and Tom was dying for a wee. In those days, in the blackout, we went in the building and Tom said to the man, 'Could I go to your toilet?' He said, 'Yes,' and pointed him the way. What a difference from nowadays, in the bright lights, people are doing it all over! [laughs] This was in the blackout, nobody could see, but it was still polite, you know.

One serious incident: my cousin Marion who lived in Gorton in Englefield Grove [near Sunny Brow Park]; the house next door had a fairly direct hit, and Marion and her father – her mother had died – were the sort of people who said, 'We're not going to shelter. If it's got your name on it, you're going to get it, wherever you are.' So they were sitting by the fire, listening to the radio,

Just 14in long, the incendiary bomb nevertheless had a devastating effect once detonated. The magnesium fires were difficult to contain and acted as guides for the next wave of bombers. *(Author's collection/Imperial War Museum North)*

and they were thrown – the house was more or less destroyed – but they were sitting in armchairs with high backs and they were thrown forward, and they weren't desperately hurt, but Marion's foot was burned with the embers coming out of the fire, not from the bomb. It was the sofas that saved them. But the gap is still there; if you go to Englefield Grove, they never rebuilt it.

ALLEN HAYES

[The speaker worked at Groves and Whitnall Brewery, near Regent Bridge, Salford.] This warden shouted to me, he said, 'There's something happening,' and somebody shouts, 'Look up … look up!' And we looked up and somebody said, 'Oh, it's a flare.' This warden must have known … so he shouts, 'Groves … it's a bloody landmine.'

I took off down Wilburn Street … I think I passed about two entries and I come to the third one and I dived down it and across the road … I got lifted off the floor, crashed down again, and I crouched there, and I could hear things falling over, and something fell, it must have been about as big as a house, and it crashed down not far away from me.

… I came out and I thought, 'What the hell's that?' Everything's battered, you know? Everything's dirty: smoke, soot, I mean these are old houses.

… And after shaking myself I was thinking to myself, 'Well I'm safe, I'll go and see what's going on.' There were still guns going off and bombs falling, but they were more distant, you know. This one, I walked on to Regent Road, I was demoralised. I didn't know where I was. I couldn't think that I … I stood there: 'Where am I? Where am I?' I couldn't localise anything. That whole building had gone.

(Courtesy of Life Times Oral History Collection, Salford Museum and Art Gallery)

ELIZABETH CHAPMAN

There were many air raids, but luckily none that were seriously damaging in our particular area; but we were always finding bits of shrapnel in the garden and in the road outside the house. It was generally assumed that the Germans were attempting to bomb the Stockport railway viaduct, which was such an important link between the north and the south of the country, and of course we had many prominent aircraft and engineering factories such as the Fairey Aviation plant at Heaton Chapel.

The new house in which we were living [Brinnington Road, Stockport] was situated in a then rural area and almost at the summit of a fairly steep hill, lined with tall trees and hawthorn bushes. One night, my parents and I were returning home very late from a night out. The last bus had gone hours ago – bus services were very curtailed during the war – and it was a case of using 'Shanks's Pony'. Very few people possessed cars in those days, and if one did there was very little petrol to spare for private motoring. So there we were, returning home in the blackout, walking up this hill. The air-raid warning siren had sounded, so we were very anxious to get home to shelter. To our right, the land fell away to a deep valley with the River Goyt meandering through its trough.

Suddenly the darkness was pierced by searchlights criss-crossing the skies. We could hear the throbbing tones of enemy aircraft overhead and suddenly the valley became illuminated by brightly coloured flares dropped by the German planes. The whole of the valley was lit up. You could see for miles! Then came the staccato chatter of the ack–ack guns. Incendiary bombs began to rain down all around us. We started to run for our lives. Just as we reached the corner of our road we heard the whine of a descending bomb. We flung ourselves down on the pavement to escape the blast. There was a terrific explosion a couple of seconds later. We lay there too terrified to move. Finally we picked ourselves up. Fortunately for us, the bomb had landed not a quarter of a mile away, although it had sounded as if it was almost on top of us.

By this time there were quite a few Local Defence Volunteers and ARP personnel racing about with stirrup pumps and sandbags to extinguish the dozens of incendiary bombs which were now burning and flaming up in the roads and neighbouring gardens. Luckily our house remained undamaged. We were very glad to get home that night, I can tell you!

(From One Child's War: Memories of a Wartime Childhood in Stockport*)*

BRYANT ANTHONY HILL

I came into Victoria Station – we should have gone into Exchange but it had been bombed – on a Sunday, coming back from visiting relations, and we went through the town, and you could see the buildings on fire.

Near where I lived, we got a plane down, just where Wythenshawe became Gatley, at what we used to call 'the winking light' [the amber crossing light at junction of Longley Lane and Altrincham Road]. It was in a field [the site of present-day Sharston Green Business Park]. Of course we all went down to see the German plane, with soldiers surrounding it with rifles, before it was dismantled and taken away. We got no bombs that I know of there, but they dropped bombs on Timperley, but only on a couple of houses, very little. At Northenden they dropped bombs, but they were a bit out with that, they dropped them on the golf course!

My father was a senior member of the ARP; he joined in 1938 when they first started recruiting. He'd get me up at night, he'd say, 'Look at this!' and the search-lights would be shining in the sky and they'd be shooting at aeroplanes. Bits of shrapnel would be dropping all round, and I'd go round collecting shrapnel and bring it home.

A new hobby was collecting bits of shrapnel or remains of German bombers. *(Ministry of Information/*Manchester Evening News*)*

DIANE SWIFT

At the end of Walnut Street and Clopton Street [Hulme] were two public houses on the corner. They were called The Beehive and The Town Hall Tavern. They were hit with a bomb heading for Trafford Park. With my neighbour Mrs Ward being an ARP, she was one of the first on the scene. You can imagine the carnage, can't you?

The remains of St John the Baptist's church, Renshaw Street, Hulme, pictured in February 1941. The church was rebuilt and finally closed in 1952. *(Ministry of Information)*

MAURICE COWAN

On one night of the Blitz I was drinking in the Beehive on Clopton Street when the air-raid siren went off. There were only three people in the pub, and I left. As I was walking down Warde Street to the public shelters in the cellars of Alexandra Brewery, the bombs began to fall. The Beehive was hit and destroyed, and so was The Manley Arms, also on Clopton Street. There was a wedding party at the Manley Arms, and fourteen people were killed, including the landlady. Hulme Town Hall was hit, and so was the Radnor cinema. This cinema had recently been opened by George Formby, but it was so badly damaged that it never screened films again. The Beehive was hit only three minutes after I had left the place.

(From The Old Pubs of Hulme and Chorlton-on-Medlock*)*

HUGH VARAH

[The speaker was an auxiliary fireman.]
I arrived at London Road, Manchester, in the middle of a raid. We were told to take cover. I thought the best thing to do was to marshal the other passengers and keep them alongside the thick brick wall. I got them nicely settled, some sitting, some crouching, but one man dashed down the slope. He was trying to cross the road to reach an air-raid shelter that he said was up a side street. He arrived at the bottom of the slope at the same time as a falling bomb. If I close my eyes, I can still see his head come bowling back up the slope, like a hairy football.

(From Forgotten Voices of the Blitz*)*

NORMAN WILLIAMSON

A bomb fell over the road there [Cavendish Road, Withington], and we'd been in the shelter, and the raid was dragging on. We used to get a warning: there was a cat that lived opposite, and this cat would always come across here, because there was a nice fire. So it used to lay there, and all of a sudden it'd get up, and go under the settee or under some furniture, and you knew that within fifteen minutes, they'd be over, you'd hear the aeroplane engines.

When we had our Anderson shelter put in the back garden, all the local women said, 'We're not having one of those in our back garden, what about the washing?' There were about ten or fifteen heads looking over the back gate – nobody wanted one, but when the first siren went, there was a crowd – we couldn't get in ourselves!

So this night, when the Blitz went off, we'd been down there quite a while, and we thought, 'we'll go and have a cup of tea', and while we were sitting here, there seemed to be three bombs. One was I think in the corner of Northen Grove, I think it hit a house there. One seemed to go off, which we thought was on Tintern Avenue; there's a café there now, there used to be a shop for gardeners, sort of the smallholdings around there. And then the third one, it wasn't a big bang, it was more of a crunch. We had a coal fire, and the blast blew tons of soot into the room, we couldn't see! This last bomb blew all the floorboards up in the front room. There wasn't a window left, apart from one in the bay window. Of course they came and put some white cloth, oilskin-like, you know, and it was perishing. It was in the middle of winter.

The water was very low pressure, we could hardly get water.

We went out the next morning, and sticking out of the house roof in No. 1 [Cavendish Avenue], just on the corner here, was the part of an aircraft! [laughs] Even to this day he doesn't know what happened. The arms on the old lamps, that used to help the lamp-lighters climbing up, they were blown backwards by the blast, and the trees were all gouged through.

I remember a parachute flare dropping over Princess Road, lighting up the whole Hough End Fields area. Then we heard the whistling of falling bombs. What they said in the army was, 'If you can hear the whistling, they won't get you!' I don't know if that's true or not.

When the factory where I worked [William Arnold's] was bombed, on Upper Brook Street, it wiped the complete top floor off! The boss wouldn't stop, he said, 'Right – temporary top on!' They put a tarpaulin cover on, and we were back at work, it was business as usual. The nearby St Augustine's church, a big church, was hit, and the priest was killed.

We'd been to the cinema at Withington, the Scala cinema, the one that later got bombed, and the manager was outside and he got killed. You'd go in the cinema and on the screen it'd say 'Air raid in progress'. Nobody got up, because they'd all paid their money. We never got up. But we were going down Burton Road and there was an air-raid shelter, a brick one, just on the left-hand side beyond The Old House [now known as The Old House at Home], and the warden said, 'Get in here!'

We said, 'No fear!' Anyway, unfortunately the bomb hit the shelter later, and it killed all the people inside. So we were lucky there.

MARY CORRIGAN

When the air raids started the radio was our friend, because that was the only way we could get news of what was happening.

And then one Christmas, it was coming up to Christmas, and Lord Haw-Haw broadcast to us in Manchester and said, 'The Manchester people have bought their turkeys for Christmas, but they won't cook them.' And then on – let me see – about the 21st, it was a Sunday teatime, and the sirens went to let us know the air raid was starting, and all Manchester was heavily bombed.

We lived high up on a hill [Prestwich] and we went upstairs, and we could see the incendiary bombs falling and setting fire to everything they touched. We could see every chimney stack, we could see every church steeple; they were all silhouetted in the light of the flames. And this went on for most of the night.

We didn't get undressed at all that night; we'd sat around in our clothes in the cellar of the house, and Monday morning we went out to go to work. There were no buses. There was no bomb damage near where I lived, but on the other side of the road, coming up from the city, was a long line of refugee people, who had been bombed out during the night and lost their homes. They were coming up and carrying whatever they could, bringing their pets as well, and it was just like what you see on television, a long line of refugees coming to Prestwich to see who would take them in.

We had a family of mother, father, daughter, grandmother and grandmother's sister, and a cat and a dog, and we took them in, because their house was hit and they couldn't live in it. They stayed with us a long time, until they got their own home.

(North West Sound Archive)

JENNY JOHNSON

We lived in Strangeways, and of course when the sirens went off we all, the neighbourhood, went into the jail. Well, at the front of the jail it was all glass, and the holding cells, they were glass, but they were sandbagged. So we were in the holding cells, and this landmine fell, and it just devastated the whole area, because there was the Woolsack [pub and hotel] there, and that's where, you know when the judges used to call for the assizes, that's where they used to stay. We used to look in the windows and there were lace curtains, and the tables were laid with the glass and the silver, and then there was the snug at the front for the ordinary people, you know, for the plebs [laughs].

And when this bomb fell, I was seventeen then, I had my dog, Peggy, and she was on a lead, and when the bomb fell, it was like a concussion. The windows broke – they just shattered really because they were sandbagged – and it was an awful experience, just like somebody had hit you on the head, and then of course we were all kids, all screaming and shouting, and I had the lead and the collar, but no dog! [laughs] And she disappeared for a few days; she'd gone somewhere, but she was found a couple of days later.

We were bombed out, but Mum said go to my auntie's which was in Higher Broughton. But I only stayed a couple of days, then I came back, and well, the house was all full of soot, but they cleared that up. I mean there was the Woolsack, that was damaged, then there was the picture house that we all used to go to, the Arcadia. And then there was all these Jewish shops and the furs and everything you know, and of course they were looted, and the grocer's, that was looted.

My mother and father, they'd been in the Woolsack, in the front having a drink, well the bomb fell, it was a landmine, and all the glass at the front shattered. Well they were at the front but they didn't get cut, they were all right – they weren't injured at all. And of course when we went home, the house was a mess. The back wall had gone. The house was there, but it was all full of soot, and the thing was, my father, he didn't care about anything, he went to bed as usual.

Of course, a lot of people moved out of the area. It wasn't a nice time.

DR GARFIELD WILLIAMS

[The contributor was Dean of Manchester Cathedral at the time of the Blitz.]

But that night [22 December 1940] the cathedral in its setting was a thing of entrancing, shocking, devastating beauty. I choose these descriptive words advisedly. All around, instead of hideous ugliness, there were flames shooting, apparently, hundreds of feet into the sky.

Remember that the old Shambles was one vast bonfire, and the wind was driving in the direction of the cathedral – wind so filled with sparks as to give the effect of golden rain.

... At 6 a.m. or thereabouts the last bomb dropped – and it dropped on the north-east corner of the cathedral. The noise of the fires was so terrific that we did not hear anything. The sensation was just like an earthquake ...

The wreckage of Manchester Cathedral after the bombing raid. The Humphrey Chetham memorial statue remains relatively unscathed. *(Kemsley Newspapers)*

An infirmary [MRI] staff nurse was in a ward when an incendiary bomb dropped down the chimney and began to set the ward on fire. The nurse calmly dropped sand on the bomb, while the other nurses covered the patients – to protect them from the dust and soot. The action was so calm that John Price, of Towneley Street, Burnley, wrote to Alderman R.G. Edwards, the Lord Mayor, saying 'If anyone deserves the Victoria Cross, it is that staff nurse.'

(From Spirit of Manchester, *a* City News *supplement)*

… The blast had lifted the whole lead roof of the cathedral up and then dropped it back, miraculously, in place. Every window and door had gone; chairs, ornaments, carpets, furnishings, had been just swept up into the air and dropped in heaps anywhere. The High Altar was just a heap of rubbish 10ft high. The two organs were scattered about in little bits. The Lady Chapel, the Ely Chapel and much of the regimental chapel had simply disappeared. Showers of sparks still swept across the place, but the old cathedral just refused to burn.

(From Our Blitz: Red Sky Over Manchester*)*

The Shambles area of central Manchester, which contained some of the city's earliest surviving buildings, after a bombing raid. *(Greater Manchester Police Museum and Archives)*

FRANK HARGREAVES

I left the police station on Newton Street [early on the morning of 23 December 1940] and arrived at the corner of Piccadilly Gardens. Opposite, all you could see was like a wall of flames engulfing the entire row of warehouses, where the Piccadilly Hotel [now a Mercure Hotel] and the row of shops underneath it, is now. There were flames rising from where the roofs had been, five or six floors high. It was an unforgettable sight, like a huge inferno. I could feel the heat from where I was standing, and even the bricks of the buildings near where I was standing were hot to the touch. Firemen were hosing water on them, and I remember steam was coming off them.

IDA MCNALLY

The hotels on Deansgate were on fire, and there were firemen up ladders and policemen telling you which way to go, because it wasn't safe. Woolworths had been bombed, but it was still there. But it was bombed again the following night and completely went then.

Exchange railway station on fire, at around 10 a.m., 23 December 1940. This photograph was initially censored. (Manchester Evening News)

We were walking on broken glass, hosepipes and water all over the place. We got to our building and it was still standing, but a lot of the buildings at the back of the Shambles had gone. Most of Corporation Street was flattened. There was a bank on the corner, and that had been bombed. You could see into the cellar and there were loads of rats running about.

(Manchester Evening News, *10 December 2010*)

JOHN BURTON

Going to Manchester [from Middleton] when the bombs actually started falling, if I can just draw the diagram: going along Manchester New Road, before you come to Shudehill, on the left-hand side was the goods yard [Oldham Road Goods Station], where all the war effort trains were brought and then hitched up to take them to their destinations. It was a prime sort of target, obviously, for any aircraft.

People say that airmen bombed houses and so on. That wasn't a deliberate act, in my opinion; anyway, the equipment that was being used at that time was totally inadequate in many respects, and the thing was, bombs did fall around their particular target.

One of the targets was about 150 yards away from the goods yards; it was one of the biggest hardware shops in the world. Between the two, they were blazing for weeks and weeks, because bombers came over and kept dropping fire bombs, incendiary bombs, to keep the blaze going. They knew exactly where the fires were, so they could direct the planes over to Trafford Park and the docks, which was a feasible military manoeuvre. But in the process there was a tremendous number of people killed.

The buses, when they came to this area, more often than not were stopped, as there'd be all hosepipes and things going across the road. So the buses would turn around and return to their destination, and a group of passengers marched with the ARP wardens. They were absolutely fantastic, because they were in the heat of it, and firemen as well, quite a lot of them auxiliary firemen; in other words, they'd received 'adequate' training, if you like. There were a lot of special constables, because all the top people were wanted at the front line.

(North West Sound Archive)

BOB POTTS

For the 22 and 23 December 1940 we were in a shelter for two nights, in Flixton.

Two bombs actually fell on us, on soft ground – one fell in somebody's back garden on Church Road, and another one fell between the railway station and

Stocks View [a row of cottages]. I was talking to the lady a few years ago, and I said, 'Where did you live during the war?' She said, 'Stocks View'. I said, 'Oh, you were a neighbour of mine. Why did you move?'

'Well, a bomb fell on the road, just a few yards away, and it damaged the foundations of the house we lived in, so we had to move.'

I never knew that two bombs had fallen on Flixton village. Nobody got killed; some people in Urmston got killed that night, but nobody in Flixton.

The following day there were rumours that a German bomber had been shot down over Flixton, so we went looking for it. It was just a rumour, it was unfounded, but we went souvenir hunting and we found loads of shrapnel which was still warm when we picked it up.

The same day my dad came home on leave, on a forty-eight-hour pass, and this is the 24th December, he came down on the No. 12 bus, and he said, 'I'm taking you into Manchester because I want you to see it.' And I remember they'd put the fires out, but they hadn't put them out completely, as the cellars were still on fire, all smoke coming from the rubble. A church on the corner of All Saints' was struck, because that's where the No. 12 bus turned left at Oxford Road, from Cavendish Street, that had gone, that had blown up. And then the next damage I saw was on Portland Street; the office blocks, all Victorian office blocks, they weren't on fire, just bombed.

Cannon Street during the December 1940 Blitz. This photograph was initially censored. *(Press and Censorship Bureau/*Manchester Evening News*)*

We got to Piccadilly and that was a bloody horrendous sight. First of all I thought it had been raining, but in retrospect it was the water from the fire brigade, the hoses. The whole of one side of Piccadilly was a mass of rubble. Where the Piccadilly Plaza is now – the whole lot, gone. Opposite, near where Woolworths used to be, some of that was burning as well, it was still smouldering.

MARGARET GREAVES

I remember going to the offices one day, walking down Portland Street, and there was an air-raid siren. I used to get the train from Didsbury and go to Central Station [now the Manchester Central Exhibition and Conference Centre, formerly the G-MEX] and walk to Granby Row, down Portland Street. The air-raid siren went and everybody shouted, 'Take cover!' Of course, I took cover in a shop doorway, the nearest, and there was a German plane, I think it had been hit by shrapnel, but it was on the verge of coming down. It did come down eventually, further along, but I don't know who was injured.

Also, another incident about going to work in Manchester during the war: when we had the Blitz, I can remember having to walk – you could get the train so far, and then you had to walk the rest of the way – but coming home, we walked all the way from Manchester. They let us come out early, and I remember walking from Granby Row, and we had to do a detour because of the bombing, near the Royal Infirmary [Chorlton-on-Medlock]. I remember near the Royal Infirmary there was a lot of damage, and we had to make a detour. It took me ages to walk from Manchester to Didsbury. I thought, I'm never going to get home. We had the blackout, we had fog as well, we had the bombs dropping, you name it, we had it! And I think, goodness me, would they do it these days? I suppose they would if they had to do, but I don't know.

I can remember another incident: I was with my mother, my father was out, he was a transport driver, and the air-raid sirens went. I think this was when the Blitz was at its highest, and the air-raid warden, a Mr Porter, a very kind man, came round and he said, 'Are you all right?' I was sitting on the cellar steps; we lived in a four-bedroomed house on Osborne Street, off Barlow Moor Road, and all that was bothering me was 'where was my dad? Where was he?' I was terrified that he was going to get killed. But he came in, he was quite all right.

I can remember the absolute terror, and every time I hear an air-raid siren now, I go cold. I can feel my stomach tightening up. I'm not a nervous type, really, but that brings me back to those instances: it was a frightening experience during the Blitz.

STAN WILKINSON

[The speaker was a private in the Manchester Regiment.]
I had hoped to be issued with a leave pass for Christmas Day [1940]. No such luck. We were issued with picks and shovels yet again. We were taken down the Oldham Road where a large power station had been bombed. The rubble was about 7ft high. We were given two hours off for lunch as a special treat for Christmas and then got back to the barracks at about 7.30 p.m.

Eventually we were served our Christmas dinner – stone cold. We were so mad – Christmas Day, we could not go home, we had worked like navvies and been given a cold dinner. We banged our mugs on the table but there were no officers or NCOs to take notice; they

Firefighters at work at the corner of Silver Street (off Portland Street) during the 1940 Christmas Blitz. *(Greater Manchester Police Museum and Archives)*

had probably gone home! Eventually the sergeant cook appeared, so we relieved our feelings by telling him what to do with his rotten Christmas pudding!

(From The Blitz*)*

ARTHUR ROBERT DAVENPORT

I went into Manchester centre and saw buildings that had been damaged, with smoke still coming from their remains. People still went to work, but 'the continuous bombing made workers fractious,' said my dad, 'and made them argue among themselves.' When it was pointed out that this was playing into the enemies' hands, it had a sobering effect on the workforce.

My granddad, Robert Bambroffe, lived with Aunty Esther [in Newton Heath], but he was very old and not fit enough to be an active warden. He stayed in bed and said he had no intention of being up all night in the shelter. If he were to die he'd prefer to die in his bed, and the Germans weren't going to disrupt his sleep. His claim to fame was that he'd helped to build Blackpool Tower and he'd put the last nuts and bolts into position after the tower had opened. Next door to us was a very old lady at No. 23, and she also stayed in bed as far as I could remember.

RENEE SMITH

As the youngest I wasn't allowed out much because of the war. We had an air-raid Anderson shelter in the garden. There was a bad blitz over Christmas and New Year 1940–41. I remember my sisters came over from Hulme and couldn't get back. You could smell the city was burning. I remember a bomb on Barlow Moor Road just in front of where the Kentucky Fried Chicken place is now. It used to be a cinema and it was burning all day.

T. MARRIOTT-MOORE

Bits of burnt paper – letters and that – were floating down on Sale for three, four days. So it just shows the intensity of the blaze, especially in the region of Piccadilly, at Christmas. And strange to say, of course, they stopped dead on twelve on the second night.

We had a little apprentice from Salford, and I was busy, seeing that the place got gradually tidied up because the blast was terrific and a lot of glass had gone, and I spotted this little lad sneaking past my office, and I could see in his pocket what appeared to be silk cord. I called him across and said, 'Where've you got that from?'

'Oh,' he said, 'I've got it from the White City.' [A greyhound track near to the speaker's works.]

'Whereabouts?'

He said, 'Well there are some things hanging on the wire at the White City.'

'Hanging by these cords?'

'Yes, sir.'

'Mm. Well, you see that policeman by the Dog and Partridge? Go and tell him there are landmines in the White City greyhound track.'

And it's a good job he didn't cut all the strings down or we wouldn't have been here today! Of course they evacuated us immediately, and right behind the works there was a train stopped. They'd cut the railway, both ends of it. I think they must have been after the Throstle Nest power station [near the present Pomona Metrolink station], but they missed that, fortunately.

I tried to phone a superintendent that I knew, at East Union Street Police Station [Old Trafford, headquarters of a Lancashire County police division], but couldn't get through, and eventually I got through to Stretford Police Station, and he said, 'You won't speak to him again, because they dropped a landmine on East Union Street.'

(North West Sound Archive)

HELEN SEPHTON

When I was one, my mum said they were in Abbey Hey Lane, No. 535 Abbey Hey Lane [Gorton], three doors down from the canal steps. My mum and dad were lying in bed and I was in my cot, she said, holding and drinking my bottle, and they heard this bomb coming down over the roofs. They knew that it was very very near, and it was probably going to be a direct hit, because they both looked at each other and then they looked at me and they said, 'Poor little soul, she's only one.'

It flattened the street behind Johnson's Paintworks, the row of houses at the back there, just off Highmead Street. If you're ever passing, all the houses on the left-hand side are old, and on this side, all the houses are post-war, all new houses. That tells you where the hit was, it took the whole row down. It was just a breath away from where we were.

My birthday is in November, so that would have been around Christmas 1940.

It was bad enough when the bombs hit the buses, because sometimes there was a direct hit on a bus, but when it was the trams, all the lines were buckled, you see, and that was out for ages because they didn't have the manpower, you know, the men were off in the army, so it took ages to rectify something like that. There was a big hole in the ground, and all the twisted metal and everything.

I remember the trams because the trams came down Abbey Hey Lane, around the corner, and then it turned right and went down Cross Lane.

PHYLLIS STEWART

I'd been to my mum's and I was catching the bus back – I have a feeling it was the Monday – and I got into the square [Mersey Square, Stockport] and there was the bus shelter near the old fire station. Everybody used to go in that shelter, who lived up Offerton, and the sirens went and the inspector came and he said, 'Anybody wanting to go home tonight,' he said, 'You'll have to walk it, because we're knocking the buses off.' So I turned round and looked and I said, 'Is anybody walking up Offerton?' And a voice shouts, 'Yes, it's me, Phyllis,' and it was my husband's cousin's wife.

So we get walking up the hill onto Petersgate. All of a sudden these two aeroplanes go over, and she said – I'll always remember – she said, 'Oh, they must be ours, don't worry.' I said, 'I'm not waiting for 'em to find out if they're ours or not. Come on, let's go in the shelter in the Market Place.' So she said, 'Is there one?' I said, 'Well, I think there is.' And there was all sandbags piled high, so we got in there, and it was very rowdy, and people were shouting at one another and singing and dancing, it was very rowdy.

I remember there were like wooden shelves, where the kiddies lay on, you know, they were like beds for you to lie on, but it wasn't all that crowded, but it's just that I have this in my memory that the kids were singing and dancing – you know how kiddies are.

Then we heard this big bump and it shook, and all of a sudden my husband's cousin comes down into the shelter, and he shouts, 'Miriam!' He said, 'I've got some awful news for you. We've been bombed. There's a bomb dropped at the top of the road.' She said, 'Which road?' He said, 'Hayburn Road.' [Off the A626 to Marple] That's where we lived.

He said, 'Come on, we'll have to walk back.' He had a bike, and because it was pitch black, you see, he rides straight into these sandbags and he knocked his head and that, you know.

Anyway, we walked home, and when I got home, my husband had been waiting at the back door for me. He just managed to close the back door, and this bomb dropped. It shook all the bathroom, and he just managed to stand near the

Victoria Station during the Blitz: 23 December 1940. This photograph was initially censored. (Manchester Evening News)

kitchen cabinet, but all the roof came in on him. He would have been in a shelter up the road, at a neighbour's; he reinforced it for them, and it was a marvellous big shelter under one of these big houses on Offerton Lane.

My next door neighbour said, 'I was sat in the kitchen, and it blew me right down the hall to the front door. We've no glass in the house, all the glass is blown out.'

When we got into the house, there was soot piled high. And my husband had only just built that pair of houses. The back door just blew in. There were big paving stones all over the garden.

It must have been about eleven o'clock at night when a bomb fell on the crossroads of Hayburn Road and Montagu Road. It seems that a lady was coming round the corner to go to her daughter's, and she had a torch on. Whether he saw the torch, the aeroplane, or whether it was one bomb he wanted – they all say it was one bomb he wanted to let go – but it killed her, and it killed a man that came out to have a look at what was going on.

Then we had all the trouble of cleaning up, and my husband had all the trouble of putting all the locks on the doors, new locks, putting the windows in, things like that.

(North West Sound Archive)

PETER ROUGHAN

Well, it was near Baxendale's [a former mill on Shudehill; a multi-storey car park is now on the site] when a friend of mine was going home, and a policeman said, 'I wouldn't go down there just yet.'

He said, 'Why?'

He [the policeman] said, 'Just look.' The buildings were all on fire, and there were thousands of rats crossing the street. He couldn't have walked down without walking on rats, there were that many leaving the burning buildings.

(North West Sound Archive)

FRANCIS HOGAN

I was in the house in Newcroft Road [Urmston] one minute, then my mum said we had to come in the shelter. It was just a big building, virtually outside our house. I remember going in, and there was this woman, hysterical, and she was pregnant; and she threw her arms around me and she was screaming her head off, 'Oh, what are we gonna do, the baby, oh.' Anyway, what I did, I got out of there, and went looking for shrapnel! [laughs] My dad wouldn't go in this shelter, he was a bloke out of the trenches, the First World War, and he said, 'If it's gonna get me, it'll get me in here, in bed!'

So the next thing, this stick of bombs came right across the fields at the back of our houses, and I think the final one, there was a big double-fronted detached house on Stretford Road, and the next morning, there was nothing there, just rubble.

I went down to the centre of Manchester after the Blitz, and it was a bloody mess. My dad used to do fire-watching. He worked for the Co-op Wholesale, near the bridge at Old Trafford, the big building there, and to me he always seemed to be on fire-watch. I was at Metro Vicks, and the day after the bombing, where I was working, on the dynamos, there was no roof! So we had these coke fires all over the place, we were still working. We were about that deep in water as well [indicates around 2ft higher than the floor] from all the fire hoses and what have you, but we just got on with it.

There was no way our spirit would have been broken, no way. We were always bloody singing, actually! I remember working where they were making harnesses for the Lancaster, and this was this guy and a female, and they used to sing a duet all bloody day long. They were marvellous singers, but I'm surprised they didn't get a sore throat. [laughs] We weren't really frightened, not to the extent of giving up, we were just normal people getting on with the job.

BOB WILD

My brother and I went down to Manchester to take a meat and potato pie to my father, who was engaged in the rescue service. The Deansgate Hotel and the Queen's Hotel had gone. They were in rubble. I can remember the hosepipes snaking across the roads, and there was a piano shop called Crane's, and all the pianos had been blown out, and there were bits of them all over the road.

(Manchester Evening News, *10 December 2010*)

NANCY DRUMM

My sister lived in Rusholme. She had been living in London, but my mother said, 'I want you to go back to Manchester, we're going to get bombed to hell in London here.' [laughs] Where she lived – she went later to see – she used to live in this street in Chelsea, it wasn't posh then, it was just ordinary, down by the Embankment, and it was gone! The whole street had been bombed, absolutely, not a stitch left of it. Anyway, she came back to Manchester, and she got a house to rent, and the night of the Blitz we had, she had a young baby, a six-month-old baby in a laundry basket under the stairs, and her little boy was 3. She was baking for Christmas – there was a couple of trays of mince pies in the oven. Anyway, when the siren went she said, 'Oh Lord, my mince pies are going for a Burton!' [laughs]

But the window, it was a big window too, and it just lifted out and went out, into the garden. We weren't bombed, I think it was the blast. And we were there till morning of course, under the stairs. If you didn't have a shelter, you used to go under the stairs.

MARY MALCOLM GREGORY

While the Manchester Blitz was on, we spent 8–10 hours in the basement [at Hollinwood Ferranti's] each night. We used to book so many hours air raid on our time sheets.

You'd have to go up to the canteen about eleven o'clock for your dinner, and they would lend you an ARP helmet. You'd put your helmet on, run up and get your dinner, and bring it back. Everybody used to knit – they knit socks, scarves, knit everything. Some of us used to read, others used to go to sleep.

I'll tell you what upset us most at the time: there were a lot of girls working there – they were Manchester machinists – and they were drafted into the Ferranti's job, so when they worked nights with us, and they knew the planes were going, the sirens had gone, they were a bag of nerves. They didn't know whether their home would be still standing when they got home the following morning.

And the only way we'd get to know would be the following night, seeing who was missing, and we'd hear, 'her house is flattened,' and they'd have been taken somewhere else. It was upsetting like that, that was the worst part of it, I think.

(North West Sound Archive)

A bomb disposal team deals with an unexploded bomb in the back garden of a house on Victoria Road, Whalley Range. *(Greater Manchester Police Museum and Archives)*

TREFOR JONES

The space in between Nos 3 and 5 Chandos Road South [Chorlton-cum-Hardy] was where a bomb landed one night. My father was a fire-watcher, and so was Mr Bardsley, who lived in the house opposite. Mr Bardsley and his son, who was my pal, were in the road when they heard [makes whistling sound of a bomb falling] coming down, and they decided to go and get down behind Mr Bardsley's front garden wall. The bomb landed here [in the driveway between Nos 3 and 5] and the crater, it was right the way round – I've never seen anything like it. The next morning we came out looking for shrapnel as us lads did, and there was a huge – I'd say from memory it was probably about 10ft deep, which is pretty deep. It was a big bomb.

We were in our cellar at No. 11. My father was in the building trade, and he got corrugated iron, which he jammed up against the roof with pit props. So down at the bottom of the stairs in the cellar at No. 11, was our shelter, which my dad reckoned that if a bomb landed it would save us. That's where me, my mother, and two sisters were when the bomb went off. What a noise! As you can imagine.

The same night that the bomb landed in Chandos Road South, a bomb landed on Egerton Road South, and demolished the house [near the junction with St Werburgh's Road]. Unfortunately the family were killed. What they were aiming at, on the corner of St Werburgh's Road and Egerton Road South there's a small sub-station which the Germans had on maps. After the war, maps were found belonging to the Luftwaffe, and it was clearly marked as a target.

EILEEN TOWERS

There was a story – and this is rather laughable, really – that went round, one of the nights when Withington got a bit of damage, you know, because I think near the baths in Withington, that was bombed there, and I don't know whether that was a landmine. But there was one landmine that came down, and it came down and it stuck in a tree in St Paul's churchyard. And people said: 'That's the old vicar!' [laughs] You know, he wasn't there of course, he was in heaven as they thought – 'that's right, he's stopped the thing falling!' But I think it was that same night when a landmine did hit, somewhere near the baths, on Burton Road. [*See* page 40: Norman Williamson]

ANN STANSFIELD

We heard Lord Haw-Haw boasting on the radio that this particular pilot knew every inch of Manchester. And it certainly seemed that he did.

My husband came home from work full of the news of this German plane he had seen flying so low over Portland Street that he could see the number on the fuselage very clearly. But I had already encountered the same plane. I was walking along Victoria Avenue in Blackley, in daylight with my son Alan and my father when the plane flew overhead. It was so low, I could actually see the pilot in a black helmet grinning.

Then we heard the phut, phut of machine gun bullets, so I threw myself on top of Alan. The bullets killed some cows in a field just ahead of us.

(Manchester Evening News *supplement, 5 September 1989*)

HILDA MASON

I remember I used to go home from work – I finished work at five o'clock – just as I got home, my mum used to put my dinner on the table. The next minute the sirens went. We had an Anderson shelter built in the garden; we had a back garden because I lived in Stretford, and when we knew about the war, they came round, my dad dug a big hole, and they brought the Anderson shelter and we built it and covered it with soil and we even had daffodils and flowers growing on the top of it. And inside the Anderson shelter we had bunk beds, so when I used to come home from work the sirens used to go, and naturally I had to get my dinner and take it in the shelter and finish eating it in there.

And many a night of course I used to spend in the shelter, because of the sirens, because where we lived, we lived on Derbyshire Lane West, the railway ran at the back. The railway lines were the target, because after a few years we had to move out of there, into Barton Road, because a lot of incendiary bombs had been dropped.

When we moved out, when we had to move out of our house onto Barton Road, they put us into a church hall there, and we had those tables in there, and at night time they used to put palliasses on these tables. Palliasses were made of like a straw, so when you lay on them, you could hear them, and at night time it used to be full of these tables, with people snoring. We were there until they found us somebody local in a house who would take us in, and we spent that Christmas [1940] like that. And then, when they cleared the lines and everything, they allowed us home again.

DENNIS WOOD

On Christmas Eve 1941 the Lord Mayor of Manchester had gone to a church service somewhere out Platt Fields. People had ventured into the city as they felt fairly safe there, they felt the worst of the Blitz was over, and there was some relaxation in the shops, with things you could buy for Christmas. There were crowds in the city centre, crowds of people, when all at once three twin-engined aircraft came over, pretty low as well. All of a sudden they saw the bomb doors open, and there was a big panic along Market Street, Deansgate; all the citizens were running about, bumping in to each other. Somebody got run over, because although there weren't many vehicles around, it was going dark, about four o'clock in the afternoon, and these vehicles had to have paper over their headlamps. There'd been no sirens to warn of planes coming.

People saw objects coming out of the bomb doors, but when they got to the ground these objects dispersed: they were leaflets, official leaflets from the Chief Constable of Manchester, wishing everyone a Merry Christmas, and drawing attention to the dangers of being run over.

PAT HARGREAVES

I could see my eleven-year-old brother John in his short trousers, braces and vest dashing from the house [in Kersal, Salford] with the bin lid held over his head for protection. And I can still hear the sound of shrapnel hitting it, after all these years.

(Manchester Evening News supplement, 5 September 1989)

THREE

DEFENSIVE MEASURES

It was Hitler's intention with the ferocious bombing and incendiary raids to break the spirit of the civilian population. There is ample evidence in what follows to show that throughout the war, in Manchester as in other cities, it had exactly the opposite effect.

'The first day I got my Home Guard uniform – I'm getting the trousers next year …'
Robb Wilton, Lancashire comedian: The Day War Broke Out

A city police officer scans the skies for Luftwaffe bombers in 1940. *(Greater Manchester Police Museum and Archives)*

T. MARRIOTT-MOORE

I remember one of my friends was captain in the Terriers [Territorial Army], and of course they were called up a week before war was declared, just in case, and he said, 'I'm going on my rounds tonight, would you like to come with me?'

So I said, 'Yes, what are you doing?'

He said, 'I'm inspecting gun positions.'

I said, 'Oh well, that should be interesting.'

So we went the various rounds, and these were improvised guns, against aircraft, and they were basically a post, a special swivel, a rifle with a sandbag on the butt, so that it would help the chap to keep the rifle pointed up in the air, and they were the anti-aircraft defences of Manchester at that time!

Of course during the war if you heard an aircraft, you knew jolly well it wasn't one of yours, because all ours were down on the South Coast. You could just plot this uneven hum of the engines, and then the anti-aircraft guns would open up. A lot of them were mobile, but there was a fixed battery of anti-aircraft guns on Carrington Lane, Ackers Farm [west of Ashton-on-Mersey], thereabouts, and they were surrounded by a whacking great barbed wire fence. [Manchester City FC training ground is now on the site of what used to be Ackers Farm.]

(North West Sound Archive)

BILL ASHTON

They appealed for Local Defence Volunteers. Anthony Eden made an appeal – it would have been June/July 1940 – for volunteers, and the order was to report to the nearest police station. All people who had any arms, shotguns, or any ordnance, to hand in to the police station. They were expecting a few hundred, they got thousands and thousands. The response was overwhelming them. The police didn't know what the hell to do with them [laughs] because they'd been given no instructions, but bit by bit the thing got sorted out.

They called for all volunteers between the ages of seventeen – I thought it was seventy, but I hear recent reports with sixty-five, but seventy really rings a bell, I'm sure it was seventy, and in any case they weren't too fussy about what age you were anyway.

The Post Office Home Guard was designed for defending telephone exchanges, vital lines of communication, etc., etc. We were scattered: there was the battalion headquarters which was in Manchester, and then each post office around Manchester: there was Swinton Post Office, Walkden, Urmston, Irlam, Longford, Sale. When I say post office I mean engineers in that area, in the telephone exchanges and workshops and things. Each of these places formed a platoon.

(North West Sound Archive)

Sale Home Guard marching down Washway Road in 1942. *(Manchester Evening News)*

BOB WILD

You could have a Morrison shelter – an iron mesh structure to go under your table, or, if you had space and money, a brick and concrete one, or an Anderson shelter. Like most people, we opted for an Anderson.

The shelter had to be erected in a hole at least 3ft deep. Some people dug them deeper but in some parts of Prestwich they filled up with water if you dug down deeper than 2ft. You had to heap the earth from the hole on to the top and sides for extra protection. The shelter was 6ft high, 8ft wide, and 9ft long. With its rounded roof it looked a bit like an igloo. My dad marked out an area in the back garden and dug the hole. It seemed enormous to me. After a foot or so down the rich, black soil turned to gravel and then to pure, golden sand like on Blackpool beach. I let my rabbit dig in it. I had only looked away for a second and it had disappeared down a hole. Our Ernie put his foot on the sand and the hole caved in. I screamed. My dad came to the rescue and quickly dug out the rabbit.

My dad made duck-boards for the inside of the shelter and built two wooden bunks and a slim, wooden bed for my grandma. There was no room to move when we all got inside.

(From The Dogs of War: A Prestwich Boyhood)

NORA MARJORIE MAY

We had one of the – what do you call them? – air-raid shelters in the garden, the one that was built into the ground, with corrugated iron – Anderson shelter – and Dad had fitted it out with floorboards and bunks, and light, and we slept in there every night, the three children. I rather think that's why my sisters came down with asthma and pneumonia, because obviously it was damp. And there were spiders in it!

I can still remember teaching [my sister] how to say her prayers, even including Hitler! God bless Hitler – could He change Hitler?

(Courtesy of Life Times Oral History Collection, Salford Museum and Art Gallery)

FRANCIS HOGAN

I joined the Home Guard in 1941. Sixteen, I think I was. That was supposedly too young. You had to go to the police station, and it depended on who was on duty there. [laughs] There was one bloke, he'd accept anybody. This other bloke, he told me to come back again. So, as I walked out of the police station, a friend of mine is walking past. He said, 'Where've you been?'

I said, 'I've been trying to join the Home Guard.'

He said, 'Oh, I'm in it.' He was about the same age as me.

I said, 'He told me to come back when I was a bit older.'

He said, 'Hang on, I'll go and have a look who's on duty there now,' so he went in and he said, 'He's OK, he'll let you in.'

So I went in and said [gruff voice], 'I want to join the Home Guard.'

He said, 'Sign here.' [laughs]

BILL ASHTON

Where the Home Guard would be really useful, although in the early days they were ill-equipped, they would be good lookouts. Whereas the army couldn't be everywhere, out on the moors, and tunnels, and places like that, they could report the Germans coming down. Communications were essential, and they could pass the message on. The object was to take them [the enemy] on – but you'd be cannon fodder – if you could delay them, anything to delay them, delay them.

(North West Sound Archive)

MARJORIE AINSWORTH

My brother was in a reserved occupation; he was in the laboratory at Beyer Peacock's [locomotive manufacturers in Gorton] so he didn't have to join up, but he joined the Home Guard. He had to join the Home Guard. I remember him coming home in his uniform, bitterly complaining [laughs] that he had to pretend to guard Denton Golf Club in the freezing cold! No he didn't like it, because after a day's work – it was quite hard difficult work in the lab, he had to make trips down to the foundry and things like that – and then to have to go out on some 'mission' to save Denton Golf Club!

There was usually an air-raid warden in the street who used to check that no lights were showing, and that no blackout curtains were leaking. I remember having a lesson in the road given by the air-raid warden, on the use of the stirrup pump to put out any incendiary bombs.

ARTHUR ROBERT DAVENPORT

Next door but one to my home [in Newton Heath] lived my Aunt Esther and Uncle Wilfred Parker, where they had an air-raid shelter built in their back yard for the nearby neighbours. My dad made a raised bunk bed in the shelter for me to sleep in. Sometimes I would roll off and land on the occupants, much to their amusement. The tiny area, 6ft by 6ft, was lit by a small Kelly lamp fuelled by oil, and there were forms around the walls. At one end of the shelter there was a square filled with loosed bricks in case of an emergency, to escape through if the door got blocked. We could hear the bangs of the ack-ack guns that sounded as though they were trundling around the streets.

There were no men in the shelter because they'd had to join the ARP and be out on fire-watch duty. Their Headquarters were on Dean Lane, about 60 yards from Oldham Road in the old billiards hall. Mr Perry of Hethorn Street was the Chief Warden, and my uncle Wilfred was in charge of 'chemicals', as he had a good sense of smell. He worked for the Co-operative Wholesale Society, and because he was a great cyclist, he knew the shortest distances and back lanes for lorries carrying goods to the various towns and villages in England and Wales. Petrol was a priority in those days.

JEANNE HERRING

My reserved job [in a bank] meant that I would not be called up into the wartime services, the Army, Navy, Air Force or work in a munitions factory. Looking back, I reckon that was why my mother was so keen for me to join the bank, but she never mentioned it. Knowing my rather rebellious nature, she knew I would probably be itching to join up. She was right. I decided to join the WRAF cadet force for something to do in my spare time.

I really enjoyed this period. We were issued with Air Force blue uniform, went for lessons in Morse code, had keep fit lessons and learnt square bashing [marching]. We even had lessons in unarmed combat and I loved it all! So much so that I was eventually promoted to Warrant Officer, was given better quality uniform with a badge on my lower left sleeve, and I taught drill!

The Women's Junior Air Corps (WJAC) was quite an active organisation. There was a corresponding cadet force attached to the Wrens. There was a parade through Albert Square on one occasion, I forget the reason, but Frank, Kathleen's husband, saw me marching in front of our unit and teased me about it. It was the nearest I got to joining the Services.

It was while I was at the High Street branch that the Battle of Britain took place. I remember having discussions with the members of staff about the number of German Messerschmitts that our Spitfires had shot down; it made headline news in the paper as it was the first victory after the awful events of Dunkirk. It was exciting to listen to the radio and to hear Churchill's famous speech, 'Never was so much owed by so many to so few.'

MARJORIE AINSWORTH

We lived in St Philip's Road in Gorton [south of Sunny Brow Park] and we had a sort of communal shelter in Lime Grove, which were just brick-built things with concrete roof, and everybody went in. You tried to keep warm: we had various ridiculous ways of trying to keep warm. One was you got a terracotta plant pot, stuck a candle in it, and put another terracotta plant pot on the top, and that was supposed to keep you warm! [laughs] It wasn't very efficient, but people did that sort of thing. You took a flask, and as many covers as you could provide.

To pass the time, sometimes there was a little sing-song, or we just chatted. I remember Mr Wimbury used to recite poems. 'The Green Eye of the Little Yellow God' – nearly every time! [laughs] That was until the all-clear went; when the sirens gave the all-clear, then we used to go home. Sometimes we'd be there nearly all night, but it did vary. You'd go home once and then it'd start again sometimes.

My husband and I, we were courting at the time, and we had a map with all the shelters written on, so we used to cross them off: we did a lot of our courting in these shelters! It wasn't that bad because if you got home late it didn't matter, you could always say you'd been in a shelter somewhere [laughs]. So we quite enjoyed that.

I remember going to Stockport to a Hallé concert – the Free Trade Hall had been bombed, so the Hallé was moving about – when the sirens went, and we

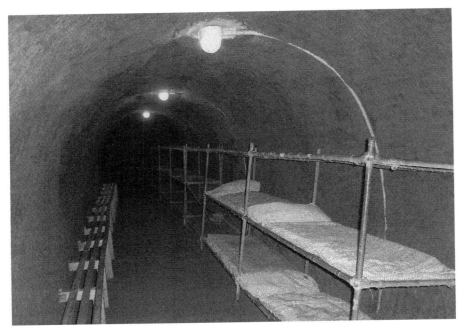

A typical set-up with benches and bunk beds in a communal air-raid shelter bunker.
(Author's collection / Stockport Air Raid Shelters Museum)

went in those wonderful tunnels that they'd built under Stockport [now the Museum on Chestergate]. We spent a few hours in there.

The blackout, if it was a full moon, a moonlit night, and it was clear, you could see, you had no problems. But on a cloudy night or overcast, it was a bit difficult getting about. You didn't worry about walking about. You were allowed a little torch with a number 8 battery, and the edges of the pavements would be painted white.

BRIAN SEYMOUR

I can remember schools having like a Warships Week or an Aeroplane Week, where you took along anything that was metal – old pans – anything that was lying around, and they opened a store room and you just threw the stuff in. They took the railings away from Albert Park [Salford], and left the gates! Every night, they locked the gates, they called him the parkie, and every night he locked the gates! And you can still see on some wall somewhere the holes where the railings fitted into the wall. Like round the church. They went for the war effort.

A couple of weeks after Warship Week or whatever it was, the headmaster would announce in assembly how much we'd made. Because they used to collect envelopes with flaps for pennies, and when it was full you handed it in.

DONALD READ

We were reminded of the heavy financial cost of the war each week when money was collected at school for war savings. We bought stamps which, once they reached a value of 15s [75p], were converted into savings certificates. I paid in 2s 6d [12½p] a week. 'The Hulmeian', the school newsletter, published the amount collected each term – almost £300 for Michaelmas 1943. The pressure to save was continuous, and I saw a shrapnel-scarred bomber on show in Piccadilly, Manchester, as part of a 'Wings for Victory' display. My diary for 25 April 1944 mentioned a local savings 'thermometer', which measured the amount invested in one savings campaign: 'Didsbury's final "Salute" total £120,204, target £50,000.' This campaign had even involved my father, for on 16 April I noted: 'Went to town to see Pa in "Salute the Soldier".' I presume that his Home Guard unit had marched in a special parade.

(From A Manchester Boyhood in the Thirties and Forties: Growing Up in War and Peace*)*

THE £1 ONION

Among gifts to Sale War Weapons week total is a £1 note from a boy of nine, and another from the raffle of an onion. Today's total is £185,920.

*(*Manchester Evening News*, 20 March 1941)*

ROY MATHER

In Longsight, near where I lived for most of the war, Grey Street recreation ground, they come there with a barrage balloon, there was a site there. They used part of the recreation ground to put up the balloon. They put billets up for the RAF in the village. There was a small RAF balloon unit in them days.

The blackout, well they blacked out on the 1st of September, before the war started. That was the Friday, when all these evacuees was coming [to Glossop]. They knew the war was coming, they were expecting it. Going back to that, in 1939 they issued gas masks, and they were issuing them at the local school; well I got mine and of course I went home with a gas mask in a little box, and I got told off for doing it! [laughs] 'What are you getting involved for? You should have waited for us to go as well!'

The Home Guard came round recruiting, and the slogan was, to the seventeen-year-olds: 'Be a man and join the Home Guard!' That was the slogan. And then the chaps who were in reserved occupations, they recruited them to the Home Guard from where they were working, so they joined the Home Guard unit in the works, like at MetroVicks here. It was disbanded in 1944.

DENNIS WOOD

I was in the Home Guard, Lancashire Fusiliers, and it was the 41st Division. The platoon I belonged to was at Blackley, at a place called the water tower, with a large assembly room underneath the tower, and that was our parade room. My father was the sergeant, and I was in the Army Cadet Force, and when I was 16 he brought me into the Home Guard as a messenger, along with another two lads who were friends of mine. This was about 1942–43. I stayed in the Home Guard until I was 17, and then I volunteered for the Army.

The next platoons were in Heaton Park, and Crumpsall. There were plenty of us. You started at seventeen, and you could be bloody ninety, as long as you were fit! They were mostly ex–World War I. It went on from being in civvies with sticks, and they got proper uniformed platoons with equipment.

We used to have regular exercises, manoeuvres like, a section over there hidden away because they had the only machine gun. They'd pass it round, Sunday to Sunday. I remember this particular time, there were three of us with this machine gun at the top of this hill, it was a good vantage point, the River Irk where it went under Victoria Avenue. I had to keep going to them, first of all with tea in vacuum flasks, they'd been hidden there about four hours. I got up to them where they'd been waiting for the Canadian commandos who were coming through – they were on their exercises, they'd come from Liverpool. There was no live ammunition or anything, but they had British Army umpires, and if they thought you would have been killed, you put an armband on and you were out of it. So anyway this particular machine-gun post had been there all morning, and I got sent up with tea, and just as I got there, the first of these Canadians came into view. And then a crowd of little snotty-nosed kids came up from behind us, and by now pom! Flares were going off, pom! – very exciting – and whoever was in charge said, 'Go on, bugger off!' and the kids did go back a bit. And then they started hiding. Two great big gigantic Canadians came up the hill, dodging about, and just before they got to us all these kids stood up and said, 'Here 'e is, Mister, here 'e is!' [laughs] Of course they were all captured, and they never fired a shot.

BOB POTTS

What happened was, there was an air raid in August 1940, we were taken out of bed at eleven o'clock at night in the pitch dark, and taken to this house round the corner. People just sat there in an unlit room, sitting on hard chairs, all looking glum because they'd all had their sleep interrupted. I was only four, and I can remember sat in a chair, cold, miserable, looking at the other miserable people, resentful at

Flixton Home Guard (44th Lancs.) The photograph was taken at the Drill Hall, Flixton. *(Peter Spencer)*

being taken out of the warmth and comfort of my bed, and thinking, 'This doesn't seem any safer than 50 yards away!' I couldn't see the point of it, and I was four!

They built three proper air-raid shelters at the end of our street [The Grove, Flixton]. Now our street was next to two farms, on high ground, and in 1940 the Home Guard were digging rifle trenches at the end of our street, on the school field. They were strategically placed, because they overlooked a huge meadow [nowadays the William Wroe Golf Course], where the Home Guard thought that maybe that was where the paratroopers were going to land.

Our next door neighbour was the ARP warden, and he was the grapevine for our village. He was saying, in October of 1940: 'The Germans are going to invade – any day now!' Well, you know – God!

I used to go to the cinema with my next door neighbour, a kid aged ten; we'd go to the cinema in Urmston, and you'd get all the war news on the newsreels, so I was fully aware of what was going on, and I used to listen to the news at home with my Mam every day – I didn't start school until December 1940 – so I was clued up on the Battle of Britain and all that. They gave the scores, like: how many aircraft had been shot down, how many British, and it always seemed to me that there were more Germans going down in their aeroplanes than there was British, you know. It was all morale-boosting, wasn't it?

The author's late mother, Renee (née) Smith, with protective helmet and gas mask case. *(Author's collection)*

Now is the Time to Ask for a Helmet

Manchester Police today received from the Home Office 10,000 forms of application for steel helmets. The forms are to be distributed to firms who have completed their fire watch plans under the Government orders.

Completed forms must be returned to the police, who pass them on to the Home Office. As helmets become available the ministry will send each applicant a permit to buy from local distributing centres the required number.

They will be sold at 5s 6d each on a basis of sufficient helmets for one shift of fire watchers only, with additional helmets up to 50%.

(Manchester Evening News, *21 March 1941*)

And the newspapers: I couldn't read, really seriously, but what got me were the cartoons that lampooned Hitler. They absolutely ridiculed him: bombs chasing him, they called them 'The Hitler Gang' in the press.

HARRY PEXTON

I was already in the North Staffordshire Regiment during the Phoney War. I was a painter and decorator by trade but I did a lot of athletics. This officer said to me, 'I like the look of you, son. I'm going to have you with me.' I asked what that involved. 'You are going to be an airborne commando.'

So I asked, 'What does an airborne commando do?'

'He jumps out of an aeroplane,' he said. And I thought, 'Christ, I've made a dreadful clanger here.' About a fortnight later I was in Ringway.

We'd fly out from Ringway and make our drops over the grounds of a country house, Tatton Park. At first you'd jump from the back gun turret. You'd pull the ripcord and when it developed you'd let go of a bar and you were pulled off. Some of the guys took a dim view, because if you did not let go at the appropriate time you'd leave your arms behind. The solution was to make a hole in the floor of the planes for the men to drop through.

We'd trained hard for six months or more, and it was time something was happening. So when an officer addressed us and said, anybody who wanted to volunteer for an operation from which we might not return, take two paces forward. Everyone stepped forward and thirty-six of us were chosen. All we knew was we were going to blow a bridge up, but we didn't know where.

(The Guardian, *14 January 2002 – Peter Lennon*)

Ringway Airport, base for No. 1 Parachute Training School. The smaller aeroplane is an Avro Anson which was used, after early combat experience, mostly for rescue and training purposes. The three larger ones are Lockheed Hudsons, American-built RAF light bombers used primarily for parachute exercises. *(Greater Manchester Police Museum and Archives)*

BRYANT ANTHONY HILL

You see, these things were never spoken about. There was a little piece of modern housing – when I say modern, built probably 1937/38 – a private estate. I used to do that as part of the milk round and then go into Royal Oak [Wythenshawe]. There was one house, quite a big house [on Beechpark Avenue], about four or five bedrooms, and if they put a note out saying they wanted extra milk they got it, with no questions. Now you couldn't get extra milk, because of rationing. But when this note appeared, they got it. I don't know whether it was police or a school for spies, but they were putting people there short-term.

They were perhaps paratroopers, who were training at Ringway.

I'll tell you a story that might be of interest. Just before the war started, they were building a bypass that passed Timperley village: footpath, cycle track, road. And it never opened. Eventually they put the military at each end: at the far end there were houses off it, and they had to have a pass to go in. And all of a sudden vehicles started to arrive: tanks, Bren gun carriers, some of them were American, some of them were English. How many were there I don't know; you're looking at over a thousand. They were parked sideways all the way along this mile bypass. It ran from Baguley Station to the Hare and Hounds in Timperley

[Shaftesbury Avenue]. We went down one Sunday for a walk, and they'd gone!
Of course, we were coming up to D-Day.

T. MARRIOTT-MOORE

At the beginning of the war there was a collection of iron gates and things, for
metal, and we were told we would get them back after the war – lying sods! –
because of course they were melted down. They collected anything they could
lay their hands on, really, in the metal line.

There used to be iron railings round Ashton Park [Ashton-on-Mersey]; they
were the first to disappear, and afterwards of course they had to plant a hedge and
wait for it to grow – hopefully!

(North West Sound Archive)

THE PARKS GO ALL CONTINENTAL
- There is a Continental air about Manchester nowadays – with some of
  the parks stripped of their railings.
- In the heart of the city you can walk from one pavement right across the
  roadway and sit in the Whitworth Street Park without hindrance.
- Its railings have gone to make up the 660 tons of scrap the Park Committee
  estimate they will get from 25 of the city's parks and recreation grounds.

(MEN, 25 June 1940)

DENNIS HUMPHRIES

In 1939 the RAF turned up on what is now the playing fields of Lostock School,
and put up a barrage balloon, to which hundreds of people turned up for this
event, to watch it being blown up and attached, by Winchester Road.

I remember some time in 1941, my father was on nights working in Trafford
Park; my brother and I had gone to bed to get some sleep. There was one hell
of a bang which rattled all the windows, and the next thing the wardens were
coming in to tell us there was a gun firing, and the gun was on a hillock right
opposite the Moss Vale pub on Lostock Road, Davyhulme. I believe it was a
5.5 anti-aircraft gun, because there was a circle of guns all round Manchester,
to protect Trafford Park. That was the one at Moss Vale. There was another one
in Edge Lane, the playing fields just off Edge Lane [Stretford], Turn Moss.

Kellogg's Factory had a Home Guard – I think it consisted of six members;
these were all people off the shop floor, and the major of course was the director

Audenshaw Home Guard on manoeuvres. The First World War-issue Lewis machine gun as mentioned by Dennis Humphries may be seen. The 51st Lancs. Division also included detachments from Ashton-Under-Lyne, Denton, and Stalybridge. (Manchester Evening News)

[laughs], a bit like Captain Mainwaring! They had a Lewis gun, a machine gun [mainly WWI issue], on the roof, to protect the factory. My brother was in the Home Guard, and he brought a gun home, with live ammunition; perhaps there was nowhere to store them in them days.

EILEEN TOWERS

If the air-raid siren went we used to go, we had a shelter – an Anderson shelter – in the garden, but my father, who hadn't been too good, he said, 'We're not going out there', so he made a place where we'd go: under the table [laughs] downstairs! I remember going down under the table. But in the air raids, these guns used to come round, anti-aircraft guns, they'd come down onto Cotton Lane [Withington] and you could hear it, you know, going off. That was quite awful, during the war.

Mr Lee, the man who I stayed with in Todmorden, he was lovely, a very educated man; he'd been a reporter, but he used to say, 'You go down into that –' and it was like in a larder that they had in the house, you know, like a little room, and it was a bit lower. 'You go in there when the siren goes,' he said, 'because that's the safest place in this house. And I shall sit here.' And he had a big round cushion, and he said, 'and I shall sit here and just put this on my head! Because I've had my life now, really,' – he'd be in his eighties then – 'I've had my life, and you've got yours to come!' [laughs]

BRIAN SEYMOUR

At first we had to sit under the stairs, my grandmother and me, because my grandfather had a small blue attaché case in which he kept the valuables, which were insurance policies, birth certificates, rent books, and so on, and as soon as the siren went for the raid he used to put his hat and coat on, pick up his case and go to the nearby communal air-raid shelter, which had been dug into the local playing fields. That was between Tenerife Street and Arrow Street [Salford]. He got the feeling that that wasn't safe, so there was a local secondary school called Broughton School, who had had their cellars converted into air-raid shelters. He used to go in one or the other, leaving my grandmother to suffer the bombs!

BEFORE, DURING AND AFTER THE RAID

WHAT TO DO BEFORE GOING TO YOUR SHELTER

—and the help that is ready if your home is hit

(Manchester Evening News)

Then workmen came and built a brick air-raid shelter in the back yard [No. 7 Perkins Street]. When the war was over, that became a coal shed. It wasn't an Anderson shelter, it was a brick shelter, with a 6in concrete roof. And they had a bed in it, and a couple of chairs. We were eventually able to use that, instead of under the stairs. But my grandmother thought that under the stairs was the safest place to be, because whenever you saw houses that had been bombed, the staircase always seemed to be there amongst all the ruins.

There was an ARP post at the corner of our street, and that's where wardens used to congregate when the sirens went. They had bikes, and they used to ride round with messages while the Blitz was on.

I remember incendiary bombs dropping in the street, without any damage to the houses. They used to bounce – I remember seeing one bouncing along the street. I don't know what happened to it. I remember searchlights combing the skies.

But they built, on this croft that was a football pitch where the air-raid shelters were [by Tenerife Street], they had built a big tank for an emergency water supply. On the street in great big letters they had painted in yellow: EWS, with an arrow, so that if there was fire, then they could use the emergency water in that tank. It was 6ft deep, and I can remember in the winter it froze, it had barbed wire round it, but we used to climb over the damn barbed wire and slide on the ice! It was never used, but I suppose if there had been a raid, they would have had to break the ice.

I can remember on the wall outside Louis Goldstone's house, which was the last one on the street, there was a wall by the side of the house, and they put on it a board about 2ft square which was a sort of yellowish-green colour. There was a notice underneath which said if the colour changed, there was gas, mustard gas, about, and underneath it said: in that case report it to the police, and it was signed by a Major Godfrey, who was the Chief Constable of Salford.

I can also remember putting strips of brown sticky paper criss-cross across windows. They reckoned it would stop the window breaking or shattering with the blast from the bomb.

I remember my mother, who lived in Chorley with my stepfather, coming home after that [the Christmas Blitz 1940] and telling my grandmother to make sure she had a bottle of whisky [laughs] so she could drink it and forget what was happening!

HELEN SEPHTON

I was at Abbey Hey School [Gorton] whilst the war was on. They started to do breakfast, dinner and tea for children whose parents were both involved in war work. So, my father was in the Royal Marines, my mother was nursing.

I remember the sirens going off, I remember us being ushered out of the classroom into the air-raid shelter in the grounds of the school. I'm not quite sure, I think there were two or three. Ours was at the nursery end, and we were ushered in there, and we used to sit there singing 'Ten Green Bottles' until we got the all-clear sound. With hindsight, I think that was a dangerous thing to do, because you're alright if you're in a bunker under the ground, but if there was a direct hit, all those children would have been killed.

I remember the gas masks; mine was green, with the thing at the front, with the holes in it. There was one blue, and a red. They were like metal, and they had these holes in it where you breathed. You just snapped it over your head like that. They were all kept in the gas masks cupboard, at home.

Gas mask training at a Manchester school in 1938. *(Manchester Central Library Local Images Collection, M09903)*

ANON.

Our house in Holland Road [now Zetland Road], Chorlton [–cum–Hardy], had an attic and a skylight which afforded access to the roof. One night during the Blitz I climbed the ladder onto the roof to watch the fires in town. Naturally I didn't take a light with me. However, once on the roof I noticed a couple of flashlights on an adjoining rooftop. I crept back down and told my father, who contacted the ARP warden.

It transpired that the flashlights were being used by a couple of German spies, who were providing guidance to the Luftwaffe bombers on their way to Liverpool. The two spies were arrested, and, I found out later, after a spell in Strangeways, were hanged.

(Greater Manchester Police Archives)

JUNE COWAN

The local Home Guard had their headquarters in Broadway [Didsbury] where I lived, in a house on the right, just past the first island. They met every Sunday morning to attend lectures on drill, etc. One Sunday morning they placed 'landmines' at the entrance to Broadway, plus a sentry, and everybody had to show their identity card (which we all had of course) when entering or leaving.

The boys had the ATC and the girls had the WJAC – the Women's Junior Air Corps. This met twice weekly: Friday evenings and Sunday mornings, at a school in Clyde Road.

FRANK HARGREAVES

Sometimes when they heard the air-raid sirens, they set light to large oil drums full of old tyres and oil-soaked rubbish – anything flammable – in the fields to the west of the city: Astley Moss, Chat Moss, and Worsley Moss [also on the moors near Burnley]. This was done to try and fool the Luftwaffe into thinking that that was where factories had been hit, and hopefully to divert the next waves of bombers approaching to drop their bombs where they could see the fires coming from, and not on their real targets: the docks at Salford, the works at Trafford Park, and Manchester city centre.

Another ploy was to have several mobile anti-aircraft guns driving around from place to place during the air raid. A lorry towing a gun would stop somewhere, they would set up the ack-ack gun, loose off a few rounds, then load up and move somewhere else to repeat the process. This was to give the impression to the Luftwaffe that there were many more anti-aircraft guns than there actually were.

JOE MARLOR

A mock aerodrome was just past Hyde Hall Farm. As you went past the farm you couldn't go any further and the mock aerodrome started [South of Ross Lave Lane, near to where the M60 motorway is now]. It was all barbed wire up to about 6ft high, all the way down to the Vale on the high ground.

They used to have thousands and thousands of tyres there and, as you went down the lane, you came to a big gate and there were always sentries there and, past the gate, a Nissan hut. When they had these raids on Manchester, they could set these tyres alight as a decoy. When you looked over the fence you couldn't see anything but tyres. The only time I remember them setting the tyres alight was when they had the big raid on Manchester.

I think there must have been about two dozen airmen down there and they were billeted in different houses in Town Lane and around.

(From Denton Voices)

DENNIS WOOD

Where I lived in Blackley, on Victoria Avenue, next to us was Heaton Park, and that was full of RAF camps, and on the Sheepfoot Lane side were artillery batteries, anti-aircraft batteries; about 130-odd guns. Now we didn't know then, but these guns all over the country were a morale-booster: they rarely knocked anybody down, but once they started up, the row! [laughs] You could hear them for miles, and we were on top of them. It certainly made you feel as if 'Well, somebody's doing something!' But they very rarely hit anyone. But the bloody row! It wasn't just like for the two nights of the Blitz, it was every other night, because planes would be passing over.

> Should we be visited by gliders or parachutists, could we be warned by an extra siren, working in conjunction with the ordinary siren, but giving off a different note?
>
> Everybody can hear the air raid siren, but will those living at some distance from a church hear the bells, especially on a windy day?
>
> J. Mawer, Clayton Bridge
> (Manchester Evening News *correspondence, 27 March 1942*)

ARTHUR ROBERT DAVENPORT

Behind the Soap Box pub on Culcheth Lane [Newton Heath] opposite where I lived, there was a Barrage Balloon Unit and an army assault course. The land was commandeered from the local parish church, All Saints' on Culcheth Lane, facing Briscoe Lane. The unit had two balloons. They were raised every evening and lowered, I imagine, when there was no possible threat from German planes. I think there was a Searchlight Unit near the corner of Broadway and Oldham Road, Failsworth, and we could see the lights criss-crossing at night.

The authorities did a lot to try and prevent injury and damage by these measures, as we were close to Mather & Platts, A.V. Roe, the Bradford Road gasworks, and Stuart Street power station. Mather & Platts building was painted with a black rectangle with a broad white line running across it on a green background; and opposite to Mather & Platts on Briscoe Lane was A.V. Roe, and that was painted green and brown to represent the open countryside: that is what they would appear to be from the air.

MARGARET KIERMAN

We used to see the fires, and at the time of the Manchester Blitz, I wasn't in town that day, but I mean we saw all the flames going up. I don't think Gorton was hit, but there was an ack–ack gun down at the bottom of Mount Road, and I think they did try and aim at that, but I don't think they were successful.

(North West Sound Archive)

BOB POTTS

Just a few days before the Blitz I saw a barrage balloon that had been struck by lightning [laughs] – like a bonfire in the sky! Burning, blazing like mad, but by the time they'd got the Home Guard it had burned out.

DENNIS WOOD

All during the war we had the novelty of the barrage balloons. These were huge things, looked like whales, made out of – I think – nylon. Anyway, all over the country, and as far as I was concerned all round where I lived, in New Moston, were barrage balloon sites. Now they really consisted of a small area, protected by barbed wire, on which there were about ten ladies from the Women's Auxiliary Air Force – the WAAFs, they were called. They had their own sergeant, their own officer – they had no men on the site.

And in the middle of this patch of land was a truck painted in RAF colours, Air Force blue, and on its back was a winch, which was a great round wheel upon which was a cable, a steel cable, and that was attached to the underpart of the barrage balloon. The WAAFs had to keep the barrage balloon fully inflated, and when the siren sounded, or if they got a radio message, they all clambered on the truck, one of them in the driver's seat, another on the engine – and the engine worked the winch, and that would release the balloon slowly skywards till it reached I think about 300 or 500ft. And there was the balloon, attached and swinging about in the wind.

The effect was that you had hundreds and hundreds of these balloons up at that height whilst the German aircraft were about. The idea was that they couldn't get under the balloons to do any low flying, because they were likely to hit the steel cables. It just made the job of the bomb-aimers in the aircraft a bit difficult, because they had to fly over 1,000ft.

It was a morale-booster to the public, to see all the balloons up. But for us kids at the time it was great because they very often broke free from the moorings,

Barrage balloon testing centre at Bowlee, Middleton. (*Greater Manchester Police Museum and Archives*)

from the winch thing, especially in the high wind, and then they would career around the countryside, the cable down to the floor. The cable's weight kept them down. We kids used to run after them and try and catch them. All sorts of people ran after them, but of course if you did get hold of the cable, you would go along with it; it would probably take you up a bit!

Now these WAAFs had to be trained to do all this work, and the place to train them was at Bowlee at the top of Heywood Road, Middleton. It was no secret to any of us, we all knew it was there, but of course it was a military camp, a huge military camp. The guards on the gates were all Royal Air Force sentries with fixed bayonets. We didn't go too close, but if you could get a vantage point somewhere, you'd see all these WAAFs training.

These days there are still many of the hangars on the site, fully intact.

JEANNE HERRING

In the spring of 1939 gas masks were issued to every household. Grandma Townley made quite a fuss refusing to try it on, causing quite a stir, but she was given one anyway. She still got ready to go out once a month, to collect her pension from the War Office in town.

HOUSEWIVES' SECRET WEAPONS

As a means of self-protection in case of invasion my kitchen poker, hitherto looked upon as a trusty weapon, is fast wearing down. I am, therefore, now practising hard at the dartboard in order to get a straight aim. I also have a good supply of pepper. I have a friend who practises throwing the carving knife. Otherwise, what other suggestions have you for the housewives' self-defence, supposing the enemy presents himself at the door?

Mrs I. Singleton, Kersal
(Manchester Evening News *correspondence, 10 March 1941*)

BILL ASHTON

And of course there were all these pillboxes, there are still a few kicking around, they sprung up all over the place. Interesting thing about these pillboxes: they were built, and the plans showing the location of them were destroyed, in case

The derelict Second World War pillbox on the A58 between Heywood and Rochdale. *(Author's collection)*

they fell into the hands of the enemy. So nobody knew where they were, except the local people, and after the war, the Imperial War Museum sent out a request to history societies to gather this information, where they were.

(North West Sound Archive)

PHILIP LLOYD

I remember there was a barrage balloon in the grounds of Crimsworth House [Whalley Range]; that was before the school was built at the back of the house. There was a gun that went up and down the railway track, a mobile one. I don't know the size

A Home Guard Anti-Aircraft Unit manning a rocket projector 'somewhere in the North West of England'. This photo was originally censored, then allowed into print in the *Southport Visiter* in July 1942. *(Press and Censorship Bureau)*

Above & right: Identity card of William E. Lloyd, Fire Service worker and ARP warden in Chorlton and Old Trafford. *(Philip Lloyd)*

of the gun, I don't remember actually seeing it, but the sound of it was terrific. I'm surprised it didn't shatter a few windows! That would be because of the water main from Thirlmere coming over the bridge on Manchester Road [Chorlton-cum-Hardy]. The bombers were aiming for the water main which went along the middle of the road, and also the railway track on the other side of the houses. They got the houses in between!

My father was in charge of the shop, the post office, so he wasn't called up for service away, but he had already volunteered for the Air-Raid Wardens before the war started. Then he was in the auxiliary Fire Service, and then the National Fire Service.

He wouldn't talk about his work, but I did find out that once when an unexploded bomb fell behind the sideboard of a house, he went in, picked it up, and carried it out!

The problem of putting petrol out of use for the enemy is an important one. Perhaps these notes will be of use.

· Sugar: this substance does not discolour petrol, but plays havoc with an engine if put in the tank in a good quantity…
· Sand: dreadful stuff, causing blocked carburettor jet. Makes petrol useless.
· Common soda: similar to sugar.
· Treacle: prevents engine starting and means complete tank removal.

B. R., Manchester
(Manchester Evening News *correspondence, 20 June 1940*)

ANON.

There were groups of Nissan huts all over the place [in Heaton Park] where people were billeted, and we used to parade by the bandstand. We used to parade in front of this – it was a natural bowl. From here your name was called out, and you were told you had to report to such a place and then you got your instructions and off you went. It was a hive of activity – the place was absolutely throbbing with RAF lads, trains coming back and forth at night.

(North West Sound Archive)

BARRY ABRAHAMS

I was born at Withington in 1941, and my mother always said the AA guns were firing at the time. I think it was probably a couple of weeks after the last major raid on Manchester, and then we actually lived in Ardwick, on Old Elm Street: No. 81.

My recollections as a very young child at Old Elm Street, was in the front room we had one of these iron cages which was made to look like a table [Morrison shelter], and the idea was, if there was an air raid you would get in this iron cage to give you some measure of protection. It was a table with a mesh side, probably about 4ft square, with a door at the front. So as soon as the sirens went – and this was Ardwick, and Ardwick did get bombed – then people would get into this iron cage with a reinforced metal top, so if the house was bombed, and the debris came down, you'd be in this cage. I would imagine there'd be a metal sheet as a floor. The local authority would have come and installed them, and presumably at the end of the war or when the danger ceased, they would have taken them away for scrap metal.

The other thing I remember about Old Elm Street and that particular area, which is just off Ardwick Green, what you'd call city centre now, is the gaps between the houses. We used to play in those. I didn't know what those gaps were for at the time, and I realised when I was five or six years old that those gaps had been houses, and they'd been bombed.

I certainly remember seeing bombed houses in Jessel Street, which was just a little further towards Manchester.

(North West Sound Archive)

DENNIS WOOD

In 1939, before the war began, the anticipation of the air raids was such that the police became fully anti-air raid in their duties, on top of their own duties. Steel helmets had to be carried. They wore their own helmet of course, but steel helmets were carried up on the shoulder. And because it was thought that immediately – the next day, 4 September 1939 – there'd be paratroopers landing, each officer on the beat was issued with a rifle – a military rifle – and five rounds of ammunition, which he didn't carry in the magazine of the rifle, but in his pocket. It was made clear that should anybody use these rounds of ammunition, they would be in serious trouble and there would be an enquiry.

Suddenly there was this unusual sight of a policeman walking about with a rifle over his shoulder. It told us all that something serious was about. They kept that up until after the Blitz.

FRANCIS HOGAN

The Home Guard headquarters was in the old post office on Railway Road, Urmston. I'd been in it for some time and we had a Lieutenant Marr, I don't know whether he was injured or what, but he came out of the army – he was still in army uniform – and he started a Commando Unit. Nearly all the young ones joined it. We used to do manoeuvres against anybody and everybody in the area, other Home Guards, and once we did one against the Canadian Army. We used to go firing up Glossop way, what's the name of the place? And I was a snapshot. Out of the ten rounds I fired, I got nine bulls.

That was the best, though: the Colonel of our battalion, Colonel Law, he came up and he wanted to use my gun to do his shooting, and I wouldn't give it to him. I said, 'no, I've cleaned it.' [laughs] He was upset!

ROY BEVAN

There were no road signs, they were all blacked out, or dismantled. All the things where it said, '4½ miles to Stubbins' or '4½ miles to Bury' or wherever it was, they all went. So that anybody that was in a strange environment, they wouldn't have anything to guide them. Which I think in wartime would be an ideal solution, because you can't have people roaming about looking where they were.

(North West Sound Archive)

ANON.

There were only thirty WRAFs billeted at Heaton Park and they lived in a hut down by the lake. I lived at home. They were getting thousands and thousands of airmen in, and I think they thought it wasn't very sensible, so they put the women in private billets, but they let me come home in the evenings. My mother got a shilling a night to have me at home, so I slept in my own bed. The private billets were all offered a folding metal bed if they wanted. Later on more and more WRAFs were coming in, so they opened hostels.

As you went in the station gate [off Bury Old Road], No. 1 Squadron was there. They'd put Nissan huts in among the trees, hidden among the trees. No. 2 Squadron – where they posted me, I was the clerk, the only girl there – that was down by the lake. There were lots of Nissan huts among the trees, all around the lake.

There were two NAAFIs there, there was one in the old boat house and they built a new one. As you were looking down from the hall at the lake, the Squadron Office was in the roadway at the side of the lake. Then No. 3 Squadron was up in the woods by St Margaret's Gate and then the headquarters was the hall. The SHQ [Squadron Headquarters] orderly room was the round room at the top.

The orangery at the side was the medical inspection room. The people coming through the park were all aircrew; it was an aircrew dispersal centre. They were being sent away from this country to South Africa, America, Canada, where

---

Jane Dawson Advises

I always saw that my family slept with the windows open, and I feel that children, particularly, are suffering because this is not possible, due to the black-out.
Regards, Mother of four

There is a leaflet called 'Ventilation in the Black-out' which would help you, issued by the Ministry of Health and obtainable through a newsagent or from the Stationery Office.

(Manchester Evening News, 20 January 1942)

they learned to fly. They were the cream of the country, those young men; fit, intelligent, and educated. And nearly half of them were killed you know, the ones who went through the park. It was about 160,000 that went through. Some were there for a few days and some for a few months.

The airmen had to be fit medically. Everyone had to be able to swim, so the ones who couldn't were taught in the bathing pool. They all had to learn dinghy drill.

(North West Sound Archive)

ANNIE GIBB

We had a blackout at the back of our house [Livingstone Street, Chorlton-on-Medlock]. Somebody said we had German prisoners in there. We had the entry to what do they call it, where they have the medicine, a dispensary, and somebody used to be without a curtain on, and when some bombs dropped, it echoed up the entry. When I hear fireworks now, I'm back there.

BILL ASHTON

The Home Guard Headquarters, they formed the battalion in Manchester, hence the reason we had the Manchester Regiment cap badge.

By the time I joined – I was seventeen, remember this was a couple of months after the initial push for volunteers – they started off with an armband with LDV on it. End of story. LDV: that was the uniform. We used the nickname 'Look, duck and vanish.' [laughs]

And then within a couple of months the organisation must have been fantastic, considering the state of the country at the time. We were issued with denim uniforms, which really were working uniforms for the peace-time army, with baggy things that went over the trousers, and a forage cap. And they re-christened us 'Home Guard', so I had an armband 'Home Guard'.

And then we got proper uniforms. We had to give in the denims, exchanged for khaki uniforms. Then we got, if you remember, little anklets, they were leather, the army's were always canvas. They must have had millions of these leather things that they'd got perhaps from the Boer War for all I know.

Then – boots. Then – overcoats. And then – I'm going on a couple of years now – tin hats. In my time, I was in say for two and a half years, by the time I got called up, were fully equipped.

Now the ammunition [laughs]: the only rifles that were available initially were half a dozen American 1917 rifles that had been stored in barrels of wax in America. We'd never seen a bullet at this stage, by the way. Then they brought a barrel of rifles that we had to spend about a week getting out of this wax and cleaning them all up, and then we were issued with them. They got some dummy bullets, and taught us how to load and unload them, and how to aim and how to hold them and so on.

But bit by bit we built up, so that we each had a rifle, and each had a uniform.

(North West Sound Archive)

The Home Guard march past at Belle Vue in May 1941, before the Americans were stationed there the following year. *(Manchester Evening News)*

ROY S. ASHWORTH

During the Second World War Blitz there was a searchlight and anti-aircraft battery [in Wythenshawe Park] situated in what is now a collection of football pitches near Altrincham Road.

My other wartime recollection is the way the park was used as an overnight safe harbour for Corporation buses, keeping them well away from Manchester during the Blitz nights of 1941, so that we workers could be taken to our workplace in town, even though when we arrived in Piccadilly it was a blazing inferno of incendiary bombed warehouses, factories and shops. Still, 'business as usual' was the British wartime motto, and I feel the park played its part in helping to achieve this for Manchester.

(Wythenshawe FM / Alex Parker-Brown)

ANON.

My baby brother had one of those baby gas masks; well, they were more like a bag and he was inside it and you had to pump it to keep the air going to him. Every time the sirens went my father had to go and I was only young, and my mother was always saying, 'If anything happens to me, who's going to pump the bag to keep him alive?' She was always worrying about that. It was like a carry cot thing and the baby was put in it and was sealed in, and there was like bellows on it which you had to pump to keep him alive. My mother dreaded putting him in that.

My gas mask was Mickey Mouse and it had like a tongue on it. I didn't like it at first and to get me used to it I had to put this gas mask on, and my mum and I would crawl under the table playing 'moo-cows'; we'd pretend we were cows and when you made the noise the tongue would inflate.

(North West Sound Archive)

ROY BEVAN

Having got rid of the burning incendiary bomb that was in the alley, I got on the bike and I had to report back to Post 10, which I did without any further incident. And when I got home my mother said, 'Did you have your tin hat with you?'

I said, 'Of course, I always have my tin hat with me when the siren goes, because if there's any anti-aircraft fire and that, there might be slivers and splinters that couldn't do you any good if they hit you.'

'Oh gosh, where were you when all those incendiary bombs dropped?'

HERE'S HOW TO GET YOUR NAZI

How would you command a Nazi parachutist or airman from a fallen plane if you had the opportunity, as one woman had recently, of capturing him?

If you could not speak the German language you would have to confine your commands to gestures. But if you learn the following words and phrases – a suggestion made by Mr E. Wilson of East Didsbury – you would be able to make your demand clear.

The translations, given with phonetic renderings, should be of particular interest to members of the L.D.V.

STOP — Halt (pronounce 'a' as in apple)

SURRENDER — Ergeben (ere-gay-ben)

DROP THAT GUN — Waffen ablegen (vaffen ab-lay-gen)

I AM ARMED — Ich bin bewaffnet (eech bin bay-vaff-net)

PUT YOUR HANDS UP — Hände hoch (henday hoch)

OR I'LL FIRE THIS GUN — Sonst schiesse ich (sonst shee-sey eech)

KEEP WALKING —Vorwärts ohne halten (fore-verts oney halten)

(Manchester Evening Chronicle, 3 July 1940)

I said, 'I was miles away. Most of them dropped on Cribden [village near Rawtenstall], but several dropped in the village [Holcombe].'

'Good job you were wearing your tin hat.'

I thought, 'Aye, whether I was wearing my tin hat or not it wouldn't have made any difference – it would have rammed my neck down into my bootlaces.' [laughs] Anyway we got back and fairly soon the all-clear went, so that was that.

(North West Sound Archive)

T. MARRIOTT-MOORE

We'd done a fair amount of scrounging, one way or another. I remember in my particular [Home Guard] section there were one or two more members of Metro Vicks tool room, and we were talking about daggers one night, and I said, 'Look, I've got a Japanese ceremonial sword, could you cut that?' – It was probably about 4ft long – 'Can you cut that into four daggers?'

'Yes.' So I took it along, and in due course we got four daggers out of it.

They said, 'We'd like to know what that steel is.'

I said, 'Well it's a very old sword, obviously, or was.'

He said, 'Well we broke twenty hacksaw blades on it, of high grade steel, and we eventually cut it up into four pieces, by using a high-speed grindstone,

Prime Luftwaffe industrial targets in north Manchester are clearly marked on this 1940 reconnaissance photo. The main south-west to north-east road is Oldham Road, and the meandering River Medlock may be seen in Phillips Park. The central gasholder is visible, nowadays just to the north of the Etihad Stadium complex. The Stuart Street industrial area is on the site of the present National Cycling Centre at the Manchester velodrome. *(Arthur Davenport)*

and we smashed two stones doing it that way. We don't know what steel it's made of, but they're very good daggers!'

I've still got mine, as a matter of fact.

(North West Sound Archive)

ROY BEVAN

There was a fellow in Helmshore; he was called Jeremiah Lord – he was referred to as Jerry Lord – he was an alderman, and at Helmshore Station there was always a [Home] guard on there, and he was coming down this particular night when all these incendiary bombs and that were being dropped and whatnot. He was marching down on his own, and he got to the station, and this sentry says, 'Halt! Who goes there?'

He says, 'It's alr-right, it's m-me, it's J-J-Jerry.' He had a bit of a stammer.

'Jerry? Just the bugger we're after,' [laughs] says this Home Guard man.

(North West Sound Archive)

FOUR

WARTIME WORK AND PLAY

The Land Army with its squads of land girls was distinct from the Land Clubs, which were more local and informal. *(Manchester Evening News)*

JEANNE HERRING

It was round about this time [summer 1942] the government sent out appeals on the radio and in the newspaper for young people to volunteer to help on the land; planting, weeding and gathering in crops. I thought it quite exciting and tried to get Edith interested, for I knew my parents would not let me go alone. Edith was not interested but Irene, a friend of John's, was, and after much persuasion she agreed to try and go with me. We kept on and on at our families until they agreed.

It was a long process applying, I had to take a week's holiday from work and eventually we were assigned to go to a farm in North Wales on the Cheshire border, at the end of July. We decided to cycle there, saving the train fare so that we would have some money left over from our wages at the end of the week. I seem to remember it was 28s [£1.40].

There was little traffic on the roads and it was comparatively safe to cycle along the country roads. I remember as we approached Wilmslow and were cycling up the hill, we heard a tremendous rumbling noise and around the corner came a huge army tank. We hastily got off our bikes and stood watching on the pavement as this monstrous tank passed.

We both enjoyed the week although it was hard work. I spent most of the time digging out dock weeds from a huge field; not very interesting, but we enjoyed the company of others. It was rather like staying in a youth hostel. In the evenings they used to set up the radiogram so that we could have a dance and the local people were invited.

FRANCIS HOGAN

I joined MetroVicks as an apprentice in October 1939. I was working on radio-controlled equipment for the Royal Navy, for airships, also working on equipment that helped bomb disposal. And then I also went on instruments for equipment that was in Lancaster bombers.

For bomb disposal — say that was the bomb there — we had a drilling machine here, it drilled into the side casework of the bomb, and as it broke inside, hot steam was propelled inside, to deaden the dynamite. Did it work? [laughs] I don't know, I don't know! This was in the research department.

A bomb disposal team in Lilac Lane, Hollinwood, less than half a mile from the Ferranti's factory, on 1 November 1941. The unexploded 1,000lb bomb landed here following an attack on the night of 12 October. *(Greater Manchester Police Museum and Archives)*

I went on from there to dynamos, for submarines. That was the last job I did, before I went into the Air Force.

MARY MALCOLM GREGORY

I worked at Hollinwood Ferranti from 1941 to 1945. I started on inspection, then machine shop on capstans. We also made fuses for shells, and 'camera control' was parts for cameras in aircraft.

We all wore a kind of khaki overall trimmed with blue, and always much too big. We were not allowed to wear any jewellery, only the married girls could wear their wedding rings. You could smoke at your machine all day; lots of people did. If you had long hair, you wore a turban, so you didn't get your hair caught in the drills.

John Warrington and his band used to play for dancing, and so you ate your dinner as quickly as possible, to have a dance in the canteen.

If you got married while you were there, and had time to make arrangements, and were able to ask for time off, lots of young men got seven days' leave unexpected. Oval-shaped, hand-painted mirrors were very popular as wedding presents. The whole machine shop would 'bang you out'. Everyone would pick up a spanner and bang on the machine. Once you'd had your seven days' wedding leave, you would get 'banged in' to come back.

At one stage we volunteered to give blood, at the donor session in the basement, supposedly to aid an unknown soldier. Everyone received a glass of Guinness, but they decided we were too young – under eighteen years – so we gave blood and got a cup of coffee made with milk.

(North West Sound Archive)

JEANNE HERRING

It was round about this time [1943] that I was transferred again to another branch of the District Bank. This time it was to a branch at the bottom of Swan Street, opposite the wholesale fish market. It was common practice in those days to move staff around a lot. I wonder if it was because you wouldn't get to know the set-up for thieving!

It was a very busy office with the wholesale fishmongers starting work at 5 a.m. and paying in the piles of loose money as soon as we opened. They used to just spill it out of their overall pockets saying, 'Count that love, I'm going for my breakfast.' The manager said that they always knew to a penny how much they had handed in and kept a record in a scruffy notebook. One of the bonuses for working there was that each week the employees at the bank were given a parcel of fish to take home. Huge pieces of plaice or cod that had come off the boat that day were given to us. It was quite a treat for all of us. We also sometimes got vegetables and fruit from the market.

NORMAN WILLIAMSON

I got a job where they were making aircraft parts; that was on Upper Brook Street, it was William Arnold's. In peacetime they made cars, then during the war they switched to aircraft. We had some Rolls-Royces. My job to start with was in the stores, and in the office they thought I was bit bright, so I went into the office then, mainly banking, wages, clerical work.

DIANE SWIFT

My mother worked nights on ammunition, at Thomas French on Chester Road. She made ladder webbing [ammo pouches] for bullets. The lady that lived next door used to let me sleep there, and I would be screaming and crying for my mother until midnight. She could not stand me. She died at ninety years of age. She reminded me of those nights for years after.

My uncle worked at Lancashire Dynamo and Crypto, at Trafford Park, on Reserved Occupation. For some reason none of my uncles or my dad went in the Forces. They seemed to keep the shipyards busy: Clyde, Newcastle, Liverpool and Salford Docks. My dad went out at 7 a.m. and came home late at night, 9 or 10 p.m., very tired and very dirty. His wages were about £5, on a good week.

ALLEN HAYES

I carried on working at the brewery [Groves and Whitnall, Salford] and of course you get snide remarks because the brewery men – most of them were older in the brewery – they never left the brewery workplace because when you started in the brewery you did thirty or forty years …

And they couldn't understand, all these men had sons and grandsons in the army: 'How is it you are not in?'

I said, 'I got Grade 3.'

'You?' I had one of the hardest jobs in the brewery! [In the assessment process for Military Service, Grade 3 indicated rejection on medical grounds.]

(Courtesy of Life Times Oral History Collection, Salford Museum and Art Gallery)

HILDA MASON

I left school at 14, in the December [1938] and in the January, that's when I started work, and in the September, the war started. I worked at Henshaw's Institution for the Blind, Old Trafford, facing the Stretford Town Hall on Warwick Road. I went there as a machinist, because with the knitwear department, they made the garments and I helped to sew them up. I was there during the Blitz, when all the roof was blown in.

My first week's wages was 9s [45p], and my spends were 1/6 [7½p], and out of that 1/6 I had to buy my tights, and any other little things that I wanted. In fact, my first

1/6, I put it on a bicycle, from Pennington's in Stretford, and I paid so much a week to get a Raleigh bicycle, which I used to go to work on, to save on bus fare.

Stretford then was a proper village, with a market there every Friday and Saturday, because my mum used to go there on a Friday night when my dad got paid. Every week or every so often I used to go to Pennington's with the accumulator from the wireless, and it had to be charged up. Your wireless wouldn't go without one, and it used to have to be topped up now and again, when it was full of stuff, and you had to be careful because if any of the acid dropped on you, it burnt a hole. We didn't have mains electricity, nothing like that.

My dad used to work shift work; he worked at British Alizarine [a chemicals company later incorporated into ICI] at Trafford Park, and he used to work 6 till 2, 2 till 10, and 10 till 6, and many a time he used to wake me up in the morning when he came off at six o'clock, and I'd be in the Anderson shelter.

MICKIE MITCHELL

They wanted women in the fire service, so I went off one day and joined up. I said, 'I've come in the fire service, I want to be a driver.' So they taught me to drive. And me and another girl were the first two to pass the driving test. It was a police driving test, it was very, you know, strict. They didn't want women [drivers] in the fire service, did they heck!

Anyway, then I was stationed at Withington Fire Station for a couple of years, and I used to drive a petrol wagon at one time: not like they are today, it was a big steel-lined open lorry with four-gallon jerrycans in it, and the petrol was pink. Ambulances and fire engines had pink petrol; they dyed it, so if anybody was found with pink petrol they were in trouble. I used to go round filling fire engines up, things like that. You'd be surprised at people that'd try to buy petrol off you.

There were a lot of auxiliary fire stations. There was one at UCP Tripe Works in Ladybarn, and there was one at Parrs Wood, near where the Parrs Wood [East Didsbury] railway station is. There were little petrol pumps there, or Green Goddess-type fire engines, which I drove from Withington Fire Station sometimes.

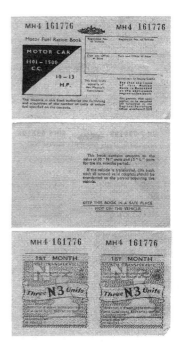

A petrol ration book. Towards the end of the war, petrol was virtually impossible to obtain by legal means, except for essential war work. Petrol for domestic war purposes was dyed pink, to reduce the chance of illegal private use. *(Philip Lloyd)*

I'll tell you what, there was a big fire in Abbey Hey [Gorton], and bales of cotton were on fire, and it burned for days. Then I remember being in town; D Division, I was in, we went to the docks a few times ...

Sometimes you'd be there, oooh, sixteen hours, when it was very bad.

A plane came down, and it managed to miss the houses at Baguley, and it landed on the allotments. It was a New Zealand plane, and we had to go to that. As I remember, I had to go in the ambulance with, I don't know whether it was the pilot or the navigator, but he died before we got to the hospital. He was burnt terribly.

The first time I ever saw a dead body was in a house, I don't know, there'd been a raid or something, in Moss Side — a great big house. The fireman said to me, 'Don't go in the room on the left,' he said, 'because there's some burnt bodies there and it's not nice.'

So I said, 'OK.'

Anyway I went out to the D.O. [Divisional Officer] and he said, 'I think I've left my lamp in the room on the left.' I thought, 'Oh my God.'

I said, 'Yes, sir,' and I went in and there was three burnt bodies, they were dead, and the smell stays with you all your life, the smell of burnt flesh.

(Extracts from the interview with Bernard Leach — See websites, bibliography)

MARY MALCOLM GREGORY

I worked at Moston Ferranti for a short time, being transferred up to Barry Street, which was much nearer home for me. Then I had a spell at Denis Ferranti's in Heyside, nearer home still.

Filling shells with TNT, 'somewhere in the North West'. *(Press and Censorship Bureau)*

Heyside Ferranti's had a government order for 20mm shells, a very large shell always being oily and greasy. When they came off the machine they were very heavy to handle. Many were dropped, and men were rushed to hospital. It was said at the time the Oldham Royal had a ward specially for Ferranti's smashed toes.

I remember the D-Day landings, when we were being told over the tannoy how it was going. And at lunchtime everyone went to the different churches to pray for all the boys out there. Eventually it was over, and you finished work if you were married or expecting your first baby.

(North West Sound Archive)

EILEEN TOWERS

I left school aged fourteen. The headmistress of Ladybarn School (Withington) had a friend who was a Swiss person, and this person knew Hans Renold. Now, Hans Renold was the Renold of Renold and Coventry Chain Company, at the top of Fog Lane, where it meets Kingsway, Burnage Lane. So Hans Renold was on Burnage Lane [site of the present shops, flats and supermarket]. I lived in Withington, so I could really walk there.

So I started there when I was fourteen. It was a very good firm to work for at that time; when it was just Hans Renold's, it was very good. Oh, there was everything there, yes. We had tennis courts at the back for our use. I used to go like on a Sunday morning, playing tennis sometimes.

In the war, they made chains – well, mine-laying chains for one thing, and also they opened up one part of it and they made bullets and ammunition. That was part of the war effort.

In the summertime it used to be very hot, you know, with the glass roof, and they used to paint it over, but of course in wartime they didn't need to do that because we were painted over, we were camouflaged. I've forgotten what actually we were camouflaged as, but it certainly wasn't a works from the air! It was probably green, because you see at the back out there it was fields and that, up to Heaton Mersey.

I was married in 1944. I was twenty-one and he was twenty-eight. I married somebody that was a pacifist, which was a bit peculiar in those days, I must say. All the pacifists and conscientious objectors had to go for a tribunal. You had to register at a certain time, and then you were called up if you weren't in a reserved occupation. My husband had been before a tribunal: I had the papers for a long time, even after he died, the two letters he had to have when he went before the magistrate. Of course he was working for the post office telephones, so that really was, for him, it was a reserved occupation. They said, 'yes', so that was his 'condition', they called it, that he kept that job.

He was OK, but other people might not have been. Because we had a friend, he was a draughtsman, and he'd been in prison because he was a pacifist. A lot were in prison. If you didn't get through that tribunal, you were imprisoned for a certain length of time.

My husband used to fire-watch, at the hospitals. It was a group of pacifists really, that were together, you know. He used to go quite a lot, at least two nights a week. Reg used to go on fire duty at Mauldeth Home, near the golf club behind [Heaton Moor Golf Course].

DORIS WADE

[Before working for Fairey Aviation at Ringway, the speaker was a switch-board operator at the Cotton Exchange, now the Royal Exchange Theatre, off Cross Street.]

When the Exchange was bombed, we went down, and luckily the head manager's office was standing, and we were all given references for the work we'd done there.

The Cotton Exchange after the bombing. The dome was later restored, and the building is now the Royal Exchange Theatre. (Daily Mail/Parragon/Associated Newspapers)

Fairey Aviation built 1,360 Battle light bombers at Ringway Airport during the first year of the war. They were also produced at the Heaton Chapel plant. *(Manchester Airport Group)*

Of course the smoke was still coming up from the fires, and Hedley Lucas, the Master of the Exchange, had booked for us to go to the Telephone Exchange, the Post Office one, to get a job there. The Cotton Exchange had finished.

So we went there and I was engaged to start on the Monday, and then I'd also gone down to the Labour Exchange, and they had a job on the switchboard at Fairey Aviation at Ringway. So I went there, and I stayed there for quite a while, until I got married when my husband came off the *Ark Royal*, the aircraft carrier.

At Fairey Aviation at Ringway, there were just two women; there was a woman who worked with me – we had a big switchboard there. I used to do 8 till 2 one week, and the other lady would do 2 till 8, and then we'd change over the next week.

We were connected to the switchboard at the airport, and we had a spotter that belonged to the RAF. Of course he used to spot other things as well [laughs] besides the planes! Anyhow I went there, and that job was very interesting. We used to have a day shift and a night shift and all men, and then the boss of Fairey Aviation got a secretary, a woman secretary, so there was only the three of us, and of course test pilots used to ask us if we wanted to go up in the planes. I believe the secretary did once, but I didn't, no.

We had a factory that made the fuselages at Heaton Chapel, and the fuselages were sent up to Ringway, and then were finished off there, and then part of my job was to phone aerodromes and tell them that so many aircraft were ready for collection. The pilots used to be flown up to Ringway, and put up at the airport hotel, and I had to book the rooms for them there.

Then of course we had paratroopers, they were in one of the buildings as well, training and jumping down. I'd fix the pilots up at the airport hotel, and when they were due to fly out I had to contact the airport to make sure the weather was OK – as much as possible, I mean they didn't wait for it to be absolutely ideal. Then they'd take off, well then I had to contact the different aerodromes they were passing over, to let them know they were ours. Because I remember once Heaton Chapel factory phoned up and said, 'will you find from the airport what those planes are that are over?' and of course the controller there [laughs] – he swore quite a bit – and he said, 'Don't they recognise their own **** planes?'

We got women working at the airport after a while, because of course we'd got less men to work, and they were allowed to go inside the fuselages [laughs] – I don't know what they did, probably tightened the screws – and that had to be stopped because, you know, there was some carrying-on with the men and the women in the fuselages, so they had to make the rule that no woman had to go inside them.

(North West Sound Archive)

OLIVE QUAYLE

I was posted to Ringway in early 1942. Packing parachutes was easy once you knew how to do it – just a job like anything else. We did about twenty a shift. If you packed it wrong, if you weren't just thinking of what you were doing and the rigging lines dropped in the wrong place, that would cause what we called a Roman candle. Well, he'd come down like a Roman candle.

Parachute packers at Ringway. (*Manchester Evening News*)

I worked on the 'chutes for Arnhem day and night. That was a fiasco. Terrible, terrible! We knew a lot of the boys who had gone over with the Germans waiting for them.

Only once this lady packed a parachute wrong and he was killed. They took her off straight away. We never heard of her again. They were able to connect a particular parachute to a particular person: every parachute had a log book. We had to sign it, and the man who took it having signed for it, you knew exactly who had taken which 'chute.

We only saw one mishap when we went to watch them training. I think he forgot to hitch his static line up. He came down and dug his own grave. We were not allowed to go any more. But they once wanted us to jump off balloons, just so we would know what it was like. But our supervisor said: 'None of my girls are going up there.'

When you come to think of all those 'chutes we packed in the war and only one person was killed through somebody making a mistake, it was marvellous, really. I have a photograph of the six of us when we had packed 10,000, individually, 10,000 each. I was there all the time the war was on, so I packed a lot more.

(The Guardian, *14 January 2002 – Peter Lennon*)

HARRY CAPPER

In 1940, the firm of E. Pass in Denton started making trepanning machines for drilling unexploded bombs. My father worked along with the Earl of Suffolk who was in charge of bomb disposal, and in Hyde Park, using the machinery from Pass, he cut the largest landmine ever dropped in Britain, because they wanted to see what was inside.

They realised they could make these machines for drilling holes in bombs, because there were a lot of unexploded bombs and they wanted to steam the TNT out and defuse them. They had machines that lined up on the fuse, drilled it out and removed it. But the Germans got wise to this, so they started putting one fuse on top of the other so, when they drilled one out and thought it was safe, they took it out and it exploded, because there was one below.

The Earl of Suffolk and his team were blown up because of this. Luckily for my father, he wasn't there.

(*From* Denton Voices)

NANCY DRUMM

I worked in a shop during the war; it was a grocer's shop, a continental butcher's and grocer's, and I used to do the books. In West Didsbury, there was a big pub, used to be called the Midland [now the Metropolitan], on Burton Road, and the shop was opposite. It was a Jewish butcher's; it sold kosher meat and smoked salmon, right through the war. We had rationing books, same as everyone else, but Mr Samuel used to deal with Cini's, in London. We sold olives and cucumbers, herrings, and like cottage cheese. Three or four kinds of olives: stuffed ones, black ones, and most of those things came from Cini's in London, or a place in Broughton. We had bread, and bagels, and that special bread that Jewish people have on Friday night, and a tinned loaf sort of thing.

We had the ration book, and they got butter and sugar, same as everybody else in Manchester, or anywhere else. These were all extras that came, and people were used to them. We used to buy rice, a big sack of rice.

The people who had big houses on Palatine Road had their order delivered, we had six order boys, with those bicycles.

I also worked for the fire service, when I went to live with my cousin, in Wythenshawe, near St Luke's, and we had to go to Mount something-or-other [Sharston Mount?], the fire station. We had to go there to train, how to put a fire out. They switched the water on, and you'd be surprised how heavy the hosepipe was, it took off and we wet everybody in sight! [laughs] Eventually we threw it away, you know we were drowning everybody.

There was a warden on Brownley Road, and we had to report there if there was an alert, for duty. We had an arm band and a tin hat, and a bucket. The warden detailed us where to go, you know, to stand, waiting for incendiary bombs to be put out. Sometimes, you know, when the all-clear went we'd go back home, and many a night we'd be out four or five times a night. And then we had to go to work in the morning.

Actually my cousin was a machinist, but she gave that job up and she went to the Co-op, delivering milk. The men were called up, so they needed girls or women to take over. She loved that job, delivering milk, but she had to give it up when the war was over.

HELEN SEPHTON

My father had a protected job, working for the GPO in Manchester, but he decided he wanted to join up and do his bit. So he joined the Marines; he was stationed in Scotland.

My mum worked nursing at Crumpsall Hospital, and if there'd been a heavy blitz within the past twenty-four hours, there was no buses at all – there was no transport to get her to work. So she used to set off on foot from Abbey Hey [Gorton], because she knew how badly she was needed there.

It was awful because if there'd just been a blitz, and the firemen were there trying to put the blaze out, the roads were all scattered with debris and bricks and rubbish, and there were bodies amongst it all, so she had to just stride over this lot, you know, and just carry on to get to work.

At that time my mother was on the mental health side, people suffering from nervous breakdowns, shellshock.

ANON.

To stop the airmen [in Heaton Park] getting bored there was a lot of entertainment organised. We had dances in various places; there was a very big blister hangar [arched, portable aircraft hangar] and we had dances at least twice a week. And we had entertainments, concerts and things in there. At the beginning they let local girls come to the dances but they very soon had to stop that as they had such a job getting them out of the park afterwards! It was a good job they never bombed Heaton Park.

We were able to use the boats on the lake, and once or twice we had regattas which were great fun. In the afternoon we could use the boats, and the NAAFI was open so we could have refreshments.

(North West Sound Archive)

JEANNE HERRING

Ivan [boyfriend and future husband] had told me that he was a teacher of radio engineering and Morse code at the Wireless Telegraphy College in John Dalton Street, and that he taught several evening classes as well as during the day. He had only been in Manchester a week and had digs in Derbyshire Lane, Stretford. His last job had been in Aberdeen with Royal Navy students but he found it very cold and decided to come south in the summer.

His brother Paul had spent some time working in Birmingham but was now home again in Dublin. He had another brother, Joey, in the RAF.

He also spoke about his family and the fact that several sisters were nurses as well as his mother, who ran a nursing home. I wondered whether he was spinning me a yarn, and in fact several dates later I did check up on him. I noticed the address on the front of one of his textbooks, St Heliers, 450 North Circular Road, Dublin. So one lunch time I went into the Head Post Office in Spring Gardens and looked at the telephone directory for Dublin. Sure enough, the address of the maternity home was there with the name O'Reilly. Although I was very smitten by him, I was cute enough to check his story. Remember, I was seventeen.

On the following Friday we went to see George Formby in *Bell Bottom George*. It was a daft film but I didn't see much of it; we were on the back row of the cinema.

ANON.

A rumour swept round that Glen Miller was on camp [in Heaton Park] and we all said 'ridiculous!' Anyway, there was a concert at night, and we went in this big blister hangar and there were one or two poorish little turns, then all the lights went out – it was quite dark – and very faintly Moonlight Serenade and the lights came on and it was Glen Miller with the whole orchestra. It was a wonderful concert.

(North West Sound Archive)

ELIZABETH CHAPMAN

Everyone used to listen to 'I.T.M.A.', a famous radio comedy programme called 'It's That Man Again', starring a comedian called Tommy Handley. It was a programme of pure nonsense, but it was just what the country needed at that time. It was so light-hearted that it did much to dispel the gloom which some of the radio bulletins of the war sometimes engendered. Occasionally the regular programme would be 'blacked out' and a superior voice in a carefully cultivated Oxford accent would announce 'Germany calling, Germany calling!' and would then proceed to enumerate various disasters at sea or on land, appertaining to the British troop movements. (These announcements were mostly lies.) These broadcasts were intended to depress and demoralise the listeners in Britain. They did not! No one ever believed what was said. The broadcaster from Germany was known as 'Lord Haw-Haw', who became something of a figure of fun and ultimately almost an 'I.T.M.A.' character. I always remember going to school the next day after a 'Lord Haw-Haw' broadcast and discussing it in the playground along with the Tommy Handley programme amid roars of laughter!

(From One Child's War*)*

ANON.

One thing I do remember was being taken to Belle Vue and taking part in a film. A full-length film, and we were the crowd scene. I've got the film and it's often on television and it's called *Journey Together.* And everybody in it bar two, I think, were serving RAF. And one of the two was Edward G. Robinson, and the other one was the lady who played his wife. Richard Attenborough was in it. The shot that we are on is just a few seconds. It was real morale-boosting film. I think it was 1944 or it may have been 1945.

(North West Sound Archive)

JENNY JOHNSON

The Arcadia cinema [central Manchester] was only a small place, we used to go there when they used to have a matinee for kids, and it was only tuppence [approximately 1p]. And oh the noise, the noise, the noise! And as soon as the manager came down with the programme, you could have heard a pin drop. And he gave us all the instructions, you know, if ever there was a fire or anything, one row goes left and the other row goes right, and of course, me, I jumped over, I should have gone left, but I jumped over and went the wrong way. He said, 'Your row should have gone left.'

I said, 'Well my friend's in the other row.'

He said, 'It doesn't matter, you should have gone left. Anyway, you'll stay until the place empties.' So I had to stay. He was very good like that.

But to get on to war work, I was conscripted, and somewhere on Deansgate where we were interviewed, and she said, [posh voice] 'We none of us like being told where to go, do we?' Anyway, I went to Metropolitan Vickers and it was a month on days and a month on nights, I forget what the pay was. I first started on floors, the floors of the plane. First of all we went in the Training School, we had two weeks in the Training School inside the Metropolitan Vickers works. We learned how to use a file, learned how to use a hammer, and then you had to use a drill, make the hole, and then you had another thing what you called countersink, so when the rivet went in, it was flush with the skin of the plane.

And then of course you went out on to the floor to work with the men, and I was underneath with this man, and every half hour the rivets had to be changed because they had come out of some heating place and they were malleable, and in a few minutes, say about half an hour they went hard, so they had to be changed every so often. And then, well, one Sunday they put me with a fellow, god and it was hot. We had to wear overalls, green overalls, and ooh it was hot, and so I took off the top and just had the trousers on. And it was this fuselage and I was with this fellow, and I know I was naughty, really, because he didn't know his rivets, and he was putting short ones in when he needed long ones. Anyway, I said, 'I'm not working with him anymore,' and I went and sat down in the old place where I was on the floors.

This fellow said, 'Ee Jenny, you know, you refusing to work like that,' he said, 'that's sabotage!' [laughs]

I said, 'I don't care, I'm not going.'

Anyway they eventually moved me to the bombsight. I didn't do the bombsight but I worked in the, you know, the bombsight's only small, I worked in there, and they used to put the louvers [air slats for ventilation] in the side and I worked on those. And then, the little window in the side of the plane, you had what you call a jig [tool used to keep drilling specifications consistent]. So you put this jig on and you drilled a hole, then you put a clip in to keep it steady, then you drilled all round inside this jig, knocked it out, then you had to put a window in, and put Bostik all around to keep the window in.

England beat Scotland 8–0: Lawton's four

By Casual

The tenth war-time meeting of England and Scotland today this time at Maine Road, Manchester, saw the visitors overwhelmed by a much stronger team.

An all-ticket match, there were 60,000 spectators when the teams lined up.

(Manchester Evening Chronicle, 16 October 1943)

Can be Done!

I read with interest of the Manchester Transport Department catering for between 30,000 and 40,000 football fans last Saturday. Buses moved off from Piccadilly at the rate of six a minute.

How nice to have the same facilities coming home from work during the week. It proves it can be done.

E. N. N., Manchester

(Manchester Evening News correspondence, 23 October 1943)

A bomb crater in the middle of the cricket pitch at Old Trafford, perilously close to the test wicket! The tower in the background is part of Stretford (now Trafford) Town Hall. *(Manchester Evening News/Allied Newspapers)*

EILEEN TOWERS

There was the Voluntary Land Club, because we used to go out to help the farmers. Now I don't know who started it, or how it was started, but I used to meet the group at Northenden, near the Church. We'd be divided into different groups of four, and they'd say, 'oh, well you go to such a farm today, and you go to another farm', and we used to go on our bikes: definitely, I remember two farms that we went to on Ringway Road; one was called Peacock Farm I think, and we used to go up Styal Road to different farms. One was Chamber Hall Farm, at the top of Styal Road, just before you get to Shadow Moss Road.

We went to a lot of different farms, picking sprouts, swedes, potatoes, all different things. Oh there was one nice one where they said you can pick apples. It was quite hard work when you'd sat at a desk all week! We used to get per person about 9*d* [4p] an hour. But we didn't have the money at all, it never came to us, because we used to give it to different charities and that.

We hear a lot about the Home Guard and other volunteer organisations, but I wonder if readers give much thought to the poor Special Constable. I have been in the Specials for three years and I think that the conditions under which we are working should be more deeply impressed on the public. Then they and possibly the Home Guard will not look upon us as weaklings hiding behind a soft job.

We have to do twelve hours per week duty, spread over three nights, to bring us in line with the other services, apart from lectures, drills, etc. The whole of the twelve hours is spent on the streets in rain, snow, or whatever weather is prevailing. Many of the other [voluntary] services may be called upon to do their 48 hours per month, but the greater part of their duty time is spent indoors, sleeping, reading, or playing. Should the sirens sound we are on duty until the 'all clear'.

Also, unlike other services we are not allowed subsistence money, however many hours we have put in. We have to buy our own boots, which have to be strong and of good quality to withstand wear and weather to which they are subjected. We also have to provide our own torches and batteries, without which we could not carry on in the black-out. We are not provided with greatcoats to keep out the biting winds or gloves to protect our hands.

I am proud to be a Special Constable. Whilst we are not trained to fight, we shall pull our weight whenever the occasion calls.

A MERE SPECIAL, Northenden
(Manchester Evening News correspondence, 20 January 1942)

Some of the farms were very good, others, you just had to eat your sandwiches in the thing with the cows and that, you know.

This wasn't the same as the Land Girls. That was a big national organisation, the Land Army. This was the Land Club, just a local thing. I wonder if other places had it around Manchester …

We wore a little badge of membership. I've still got it, somewhere.

[An extract from the 1942 film *Start a Land Club* – available on the website www.movinghistory.ac.uk – explains the organisation and workings of the clubs.]

A Land Club badge. *(Eileen Towers)*

FRANCIS HOGAN

I remember one night, we were coming home from a dance, and all the lights went out; it was the blackout, and there was this drunkard on the opposite side of the road, and he shouts at the top of his voice, 'I've gone blind! I've gone blind! Help me, I've gone blind!' [laughs]

We said, 'OK mate, right you are.'

Auxiliary Fire Service members enjoy a cuppa on Christmas Day 1940. *(Manchester Evening News)*

MICKIE MITCHELL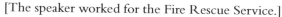

[The speaker worked for the Fire Rescue Service.]

There was a house we went to, and there was three old men there, with, you know, caps on and nightshirts, and they wouldn't come down from upstairs. The house next door was blazing; they wouldn't come down, they were sleeping three in a bed in the attic upstairs. We had to knock them out to carry them down! [laughs] I was in stitches, me, these poor old men in long nightshirts! We had to carry them down, we couldn't get them to walk down the ladder, or try and get them down the stairs. Oh no, it was hilarious.

When we was at Withington Fire Station you had a lot of waiting at one time, and then sometimes you'd be out all day and all night. We were sat there one night playing cards for money, which was forbidden of course, and the D.O. [Divisional Officer] came in one day, so I sat on the chair on the money like that, and he wasn't daft because he'd been a fireman and he knew what we were up to. He said, 'Go in the duty room and get my log book.'

So I said to one of the girls, 'Do you want to go and get his log book?'

He said, 'I order you to do it!'

We used to get fined.

Another time, driving the petrol wagon alongside the [Southern] cemetery, a great marvellous puddle of water there all over the road, and I thought, 'Ooh I'll go through this', and I didn't see anything, ooh splash it was marvellous. I get back to the fire station and they said, 'The police want to see you.'

So I said, 'Why?' A woman was passing and I'd drowned her and I didn't notice! I got fined 10s [50p] for that, because she took me to court, and then I had to pay for her cleaning.

DORIS WADE

[The speaker worked six hours a day at Fairey Aviation (Ringway) [See page 98] and the rest of the day worked on the wards at Manchester Royal Infirmary.]

I was an auxiliary nurse. We had to do 100 hours on whichever ward the matron sent us to. She'd see that we'd got the caps on the right way, and so forth, and then when we'd done the 100 hours we were asked which ward we'd like to go on. So I chose S2 Male, because it was more interesting, being surgical work and not medical. And also I was allowed to go into quite a few of the operations there. I was on that ward for over two years, and the sister was called Jessie Matthews. I'll always remember that!

And of course the matron was real old type, you know, in those days, she'd come round and we'd give one another the wire, you know, when she was leaving one ward for the next, and we'd have to take all the magazines and books off the beds, make the patients sit there just so: 'What are you doing?'

'Oh the matron's coming.' [laughs]

We had all sorts of jobs. One of the jobs was to put a loincloth on a man [laughs] – that was rather embarrassing! We'd practised while we were training, and of course we had a written exam as well, and helping the nurses generally. When I watched the operations, I was allowed to put the iodine on at the end.

(North West Sound Archive)

MARY CORRIGAN

My sister and I joined the ATS, but we never left home, because we were in the Army Pay Corps, and the offices were quite near to where we lived, but there were certain restrictions. We had to wear khaki uniform all the time: tunic and

David Appleyard's enamelled cast-iron sculptures 'Factory Girls' (installed 2011) commemorate the achievements of women workers at Metropolitan Vickers during the Second World War. They are on East Wharf, Salford Quays, with the Manchester Ship Canal and the Imperial War Museum North in the background. *(Author's collection)*

skirt, blouse and tie, and a cap, and you also had a greatcoat for the very cold weather, and khaki gloves, woollen gloves.

To go into the city, we had to have an army pass, because you could be stopped by an officer, who would want to know why you were in Manchester, and of course if you could show a pass, you were alright. If you couldn't show a pass, you were put on a charge.

Strange to say, although it was blackout and there wasn't a light anywhere, you weren't nervous on the streets like you are today. Everybody was friendly and nice. Because everybody was in the same boat; we were all working for peace, and you felt friends with everybody.

(North West Sound Archive)

FIVE

RATIONING

Before the outbreak of war in 1939, Britain imported well over half of its essential foodstuffs. Shipping bound for the UK was a prime enemy target, so serious shortages forced Britain into a system of strictly limited domestic supply. Basic foods were rationed

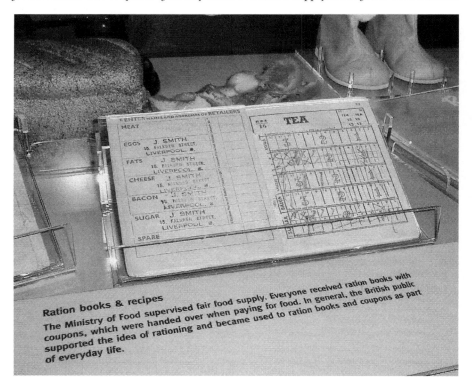

Ration books & recipes
The Ministry of Food supervised fair food supply. Everyone received ration books with coupons, which were handed over when paying for food. In general, the British public supported the idea of rationing and became used to ration books and coupons as part of everyday life.

A close-up of a display from the Imperial War Museum North, Salford Quays. *(Author's collection / Imperial War Museum North) from January 1940, clothing by June 1941, and by July 1942 petrol, by law, was to be used for essential services only. UK rationing in one form or another lasted until 1954.*

HILDA MASON

They gave you a ration book, and in it was how much butter and sugar. There was a book for food, one for clothing, and if you were lucky enough to have a car, one for petrol. It's surprising: my mum was a very good manager, she'd been brought up that way, and we never really went short. I mean, we very rarely saw an egg – it was dried egg. We were very lucky; we had parents who were very good and who looked after us.

Really, we just got on with life, and I'm still here today, so all the rations and what we lived on, didn't do us any harm. I'm still here and still – touch wood – pretty fit.

PHILIP LLOYD

The shopkeeper clipped one of the little tickets out of the ration book every time you bought whatever it was. The shops that you were registered with were in the front, so you had to go to those shops. You were told to use marked coupons at a certain time or for certain things. Somewhere it says: 'Do nothing with this page until told what to do.'

DENNIS WOOD

Actually it was a healthy diet. The incidence of heart attack almost disappeared for the six years of the war, and later because rationing was still on until about 1953. Nevertheless, we had to get used to it.

In the police station on Mill Street [Bradford, central Manchester] they used to get the prisoners' meals from the café down the road – the British Café it was called – and it would be good enough grub, you know, potatoes, like potato mash, Spam or corned beef, gravy, quite tasty. Anyway the sergeant on duty would come in with his sandwiches that his wife had made; nothing special, black bread and dripping, and he'd ask, 'what are they having down there?' and more often than not order a swap!

JEANNE HERRING

Usually I took sandwiches for lunch, but once a week mother gave me 1s 3d threepence [approximately 6p] to eat out. She said it would be an educating experience for me to watch other people ordering their meal. There was not much choice because of food rationing: maybe soup and a roll and beans on toast or fish and chips.

I cannot remember ever having a meal out with the family, but Auntie Gertie treated me once to the pictures and a fish and chip meal at the Odeon on Oxford Road. The café was in the basement of the cinema. I must have been about eleven or twelve, and when we got home Auntie Gertie said, 'Do you know what the dear girl said, Annie? Can I have as much tomato ketchup as I like?' Mother laughed but I didn't think it was funny, for she restricted our portion at home.

DENNIS HUMPHRIES

One of the other considerations that came along as soon as the war started was a thing called rationing, which meant you had to go to the shops with your book, with your coupons. One of my jobs on finishing school, since my mother was working and my brother was working, I had to take my mother's shopping bag and get in the queue at the local grocery store, so that when mother came home from work, she'd get straight in there, and have my place in the queue, so she didn't have to wait too long.

I don't remember any black market activity, except that once I sold my sweet coupons – only once! [laughs] I was only eleven at the time!

MARJORIE AINSWORTH

It came very gradually, because they had to organise all the ration books, and you had to register with a butcher and a grocer. You'd get your weekly rations: you'd get 3*d* [1p] worth of meat, which wasn't very much, and occasionally you would get an extra sausage. At the grocer you got your butter, eggs, bacon; all the things that were rationed. For everything else you used to queue. Queuing was quite a feature. If you saw a queue, you automatically got into it [laughs] but you didn't really know what you were going to get at the other end! But it didn't matter: it could have been a bread queue or a potato queue or even a cigarette queue. Sweets were rationed, but you didn't have to register for those, you just went there.

There were recipes; people used to try the oddest things. I know when we finally got married, my mother-in-law used to make some little buns, and if she didn't have any margarine or butter or lard, she would use liquid paraffin as the shortening! [laughs] They were quite nice actually.

We were never lucky enough to know anybody who was involved in the black market, but we used to get, we had an uncle in Australia; he used to send food parcels to his sister, and occasionally we'd get a food parcel. How that was arranged I don't know, but they would come from Australia.

We had horse meat, I remember, there was a horsemeat butcher on Corporation Street [Gorton] opposite the Co-op bank. We occasionally got a bit of pork, and I remember eating whale meat, but I can't remember where we got it from, it certainly wasn't the butcher's. There must have been a whale meat queue somewhere! [laughs]

I remember one of the girls in the railway office lived on a farm somewhere outside Stockport, and she invited us back for tea one day, and it was amazing: we all had two very fresh boiled eggs, with toast and butter. That seemed to be like a feast.

There were restaurants open, but you could only spend I think up to five pounds, which was a lot of money in those days. The thing that saved most people was the chip shop. They weren't rationed, so at a pinch you could always have fish and chips somewhere. It was beef dripping that they used in those days, not fancy oil. They tasted better with beef dripping.

PHYLLIS STEWART

We were rationed: there was my father-in-law, my mother-in-law, Pamela [baby daughter] and me. Arnold, my husband, was stationed outside York and you know what he used to do? He used to go around to these farms and help them to mend the fences and that, and they used to give him eggs, and he used to bring the eggs home. He'd have a little case,

(Manchester Evening News)

A dried eggs recipe list.
(Manchester Evening News)

and he used to wrap each egg in newspaper. He'd bring about a dozen eggs home every time he came on leave, it was lovely.

I don't know if my mother-in-law was more pleased to see him or the eggs!

(North West Sound Archive)

HELEN SEPHTON

I remember the egg powder, and the potato powder, that was called Pom, and now it's gone full circle because you can get Smash now, can't you, in the shops? It was like that, but inferior.

I remember the rationing books: if you had the money, you hadn't got the coupons, and if you had the coupons, you hadn't got the money. We had a man in the neighbourhood, this old guy, and he used to treat all the children in the area in rota, because he never used his sweet coupon; he always gave it away to the families with children, so we could have a quarter of sweets to share out.

JOAN CONSTABLE

I remember a greengrocer's near where I lived [Chorlton-cum-Hardy], and one day the word went round that there were bananas there. I can still see all the women running down the road with their ration books.

I remember a family used to keep a pig in their back garden and people used to give it their leftovers, and when it was killed we were all given a little bit.

BRYANT ANTHONY HILL

In Wythenshawe, I'll tell you, there was one or two that got caught. They were slaughtering pigs, and leaving them in the bath, in brine! And I know of at least two episodes of that. That was illegal, you can't go killing pigs and sticking them in Corporation [housing]… if you've ever read the regulations the Corporation had, you weren't even allowed to own a motorbike and sidecar.

They used to have pig clubs, you know, in the war. A group would get together and perhaps have a little pig, and you gave your bacon ration up, and you got a certain allowance to keep a pig, or two pigs, depending on how well off you were. And then as each pig came to be slaughtered, that was divided between the pig club. The government encouraged that.

I know a customer of my father's got caught dealing in cloth. She managed to get hold of clothes from somewhere, and sold them on the black market, for probably a bit more than they were worth. Where she was getting them from, she never said; in court she wouldn't say. She got twelve months.

JOHN PEARSON

[The speaker's mother ran a corner shop in Droylsden.]

The butter came in a lump, and it all had to be cut up, and of course you would cut it in microscopic amounts of butter! I remember one lady came in and she had a butter ration on a slice of bread, and she said, 'I had one good slice out of that!'

I don't think anybody really went hungry in the war, but the meals were a bit hard. I remember once at Audenshaw Grammar School, we had 'bone pie' [laughs], we only ever had it once. It consisted of bones and pastry, and there must have been some meat on the bone, but it was essentially bone pie.

(*Manchester Evening News, October 1942*)

You had the coupons for sweets. You could go anywhere with the sweet coupons, you weren't registered; but for sugar and butter you were of course registered at a particular shop, and you had your ration book stamped. But with sweets you had coupons and you could give them in anyhow.

(*North West Sound Archive*)

ANON.

During rationing I remember going in Duckworth's, which was a grocer's shop, and the sugar was in big bags ready to be weighed out into blue bags. The butter – I think you were allowed half a pound of butter, and 10*d* [approximately 4p]

> 'Did you ask that new girl at the grocer's if they had any gelatine?'
> 'I did, but she said, "You can't kid me." She said she knew all about the thing they used in the French Revolution.'
>
> (*Manchester Evening News, 7 May 1945*)

of meat. You got a small packet of tea, and I don't think you got cheese every week. Flour you got, because my mum made my dad a pudding every day and I don't know how she did it.

Every week in the paper there would be a recipe so you could manage; Woolton Pie and Spartan Christmas Pudding. Woolton Pie was a vegetable pie and it was really very good. You had to make do and mend.

(North West Sound Archive)

Jam! You should hear what my husband calls it. It won't stick two pieces of bread together and even the children don't like it. When I see a bit of plum in the so-called plum jam they are selling, I'll buy it. It's all liquid.

(Manchester City News correspondence, 19 May 1944)

There came the era of substitutes – 'egg' powder which had never been near a hen, 'gelatine' which was practically industrial glue, 'blanc-mange' which was little more than coloured and flavoured flour, sweetening agents which owed everything to the coal from which saccharine is made, and owed nothing to cane or beet from which sugar comes, metal polish which wouldn't, starch which didn't.

· The great cigarette famine brought the first 'No ...' notices, which grew with the months to 'No cigarettes ... no matches ... no beer ... no chocolates ... no saccharine.'

· Paper became scarce and everything – or nearly everything – was brought home in string bags which revealed our most intimate secrets to any passer who cared to look twice. And – nearly the last straw – they took away our clothes!

· Remember that Sunday morning when we woke up to find those margarine coupons stood for dresses ... and coats ... and shoes? Remember how everybody wailed, 'Why only last week I was going to buy ... but...'

· Then began the everlasting search for fully-fashioned stockings, the beginning of the bare leg vogue and stains for them which brought to mind woad-bedecked cave women. We went hatless, too, or wore those interminable turbans because millinery buying was such a financial embarrassment.

· And we got nearer and nearer to hysterics when shop assistants kept repeating that most maddening of all phrases, 'Don't you know there's a war on?'

(Manchester Evening Chronicle, 2 May 1945)

JANE DAWSON ADVISES

I have relatives in Ireland who are worried about me, and have sent me a gift of a hamper which contains some of our rationed foods. Am I in order accepting this, or ought I to send it back again?

It is in order for you to accept this present, as it was unsolicited. If you were to ask for gifts of rationed food, or to offer payment for them, you would, however, be breaking the rules of the Rationing Order.

(Manchester Evening News, *20 March 1941*)

FRANCIS HOGAN

We were always short of eggs. My dad bought some little chicks, and we had a boiler in the kitchen, and he put these chicks in this box and covered it with wire netting. We had a dog – it was a hard dog – and I came home from work, and the wire netting had come off the top of the box, and our dog was in the middle of this box, with all these chicks sat on top of him. [laughs] Anyway, they grew up, and they were all cocks! [laughs] All the neighbours were complaining about the 'cock-a-doodle-doo!' So no eggs! I remember one afternoon my mum had been feeding them, and one of them must have flew at her, and she came in and she said, 'I'm sure those are not hens.'

MARGARET KIERMAN

[At the outbreak of war the speaker lived as a teenager in her parents' corner shop in Gorton.]

They had to put blackout curtaining everywhere. And then of course things did become a bit difficult to get. Cigarettes were rationed, and fortunately we dealt direct with both Player's and Will's, so we were quite fortunate.

And of course toys were limited; well virtually everything that you sold became shorter and shorter. But there were always newspapers and comics.

There was some black marketeering – in fact, my father did from time to time get some leather goods, which he didn't ask where they came from! He felt after rather guilty about it; nevertheless people were so pleased to get them, so I don't know whether it was wrong or not [laughs], but it gave pleasure to a lot of people.

(North West Sound Archive)

ANON.

We used to get our rations from the Co-op in Bridge Street [Ramsbottom] and I can remember the list started butter, sugar, tea, marge, cooking fat, matches, cigarettes. We were all right; we were never hungry, we made the most of it. As for clothing we had a lot of hand-me-downs and we were glad of them.

With rationing I used to queue for hours with my mother. I remember once we queued for about three hours and my mother managed to get two bananas, which I'd never seen before. As a treat she gave one to me and I hated it – I'd eaten it with the skin on!

(North West Sound Archive)

BRIAN SEYMOUR

On Great Clowes Street [Salford] they built an emergency kitchen, which was there after the war. Because when I went to work in education, before I did National Service, there was a department there, a school meals department, and the woman who was in charge of that department was also in charge of these emergency kitchens. People could go and for, I don't know, a shilling, a couple of shillings, they'd get a two-course meal. That happened during the war for people who had been bombed out.

I can remember my grandmother, when it got to the end of summer, storing apples in the loft in boxes with newspapers so they would last, and potatoes too. She used to keep them dark, in the loft.

FRANK ELSON

It was simply the normal way of living. I knew nothing else.

For instance, my mother had a Mrs Beeton cookery book. In it were pictures of butchers' shops with meat hanging up all around. I didn't believe the book because I knew what a butcher's shop looked like: an empty window and nothing hanging up. I asked my mother why the pictures were wrong and she said it was because of the war, but I don't really think she explained what war was. Rationing was just a fact of life.

… I remember tanks from the Beaumont Road maintenance unit parked in four rows from Wigan Road to Chorley New Road [Deane, West Bolton]. There was a hut for the people who worked there and we used to go to scrounge sweets and chocolate off them and there were barrage balloons in the sky, but then I don't remember them not being there! [During the war the entire length of Beaumont Road was closed, and used as a storage depot.]

… We had a food parcel once from America; maybe my mother got it because she was a widow, but I remember a huge block of Rockwood's chocolate was in it. It had ridges across it, not squares.

(From World War II — An Account of Local Stories*)*

ANNIE GIBB

I remember rationing: dried egg from America, and Spam.

I'll tell you a funny story about rationing. The bacon was so short, part of the war, that you got one ounce a week. So this family of five that I knew, they lived on Kirkmanshulme Lane, they got ten ounces of bacon for the family, just this one fortnight, and they had a greyhound, it had been on the trap but I don't think it was a very good one, and it went in this cupboard and ate the bacon ration. My dad said, 'I'd have ate the ★★★★ dog!'

We'd have the odd egg, we got a little bit of butter – about two ounces of butter a week – sugar, so much a week. Bread was eventually rationed, but you just got like the main things, like bacon. Meat was rationed, everything was rationed. You got points for tinned food, and you got like stamps in a book, and when you'd gone through them, that was it. We seemed to do well for apples and plums, things like that. Children who lived near to where there were fruit trees were drafted in to collect the fruit.

There were spivs, and ways of getting round the rationing. I did hear that somebody thought one night (it was late), 'I'll go in and I'll drink some of that milk out of that churn.' And when he went to open the lid, there was a side of bacon hidden in it! I don't know if that's true, but I can believe it.

My dad used to bring stuff home, I don't know if other people used to do it. He used to put rice pudding in a milk bottle and bring it home. He couldn't let food be wasted.

I've got some friends in Scotland, and he told me that they used to go on the tip looking for the clearance of the bomb sites. Now any food that my uncle found in the bomb site, he brought it home squashed and battered. So he used to eat anything anybody found in the rubbish.

WILLIAM CUNNINGHAM

Shortages were sometimes met with creativity. Mr Shaw's wife was in a nursing home, and he had me cut up sheets of the tissue paper used for packing [at George Shaw's hat material factory on Market Street, Denton] into small squares. These he would deliver to his wife for toilet paper. To put this into a proper context, many families were using torn up newspapers for that purpose. To them, the cut-up tissue paper would have seemed quite luxurious.

(From Denton Voices*)*

JENNY JOHNSON

I remember rationing, oh yes, but there's way and means, isn't there? And my father was a seaman, you see, and when he was between ships he worked with an ostler, you know with horses, and of course they used to go in pubs and they'd meet all these people and so we were never really short of food or anything. This man he used to work at Sisson's that used to be in St Anne's Square, a very posh cake shop, and he used to bring the cakes. And my uncle used to work in the Grosvenor [former hotel on Deansgate], and he used to bring bits of food home, you know. We had lots of contacts, so we did very well really.

MICKIE MITCHELL

We weren't so bad in the Fire Service, because we got our meals, you know.

There was loads of black market. When we were on our second tour of duty we used to go to the Ritz, you know, you got two hours' short leave; we went to the Ritz dancing. I don't know where they got it from, I think America or somewhere, tins of butter, and my mother loved butter. So I got one like that and took it home, and she said, 'Where've you got it from?'

I said, 'I'm not telling you!' Because she was very very, you know, perfect, my mother, sort of thing.

JANE DAWSON ADVISES

Is there any way in which one can recover lost clothing coupons? My little boy got hold of my handbag, took out my new card which I had just got, and tore it into tiny pieces! My husband says that under no circumstances can lost coupons be replaced.

Mrs. H.

I hope you kept the pieces! You should take them to your nearest Citizens' Advice Bureau – where they will give you the necessary form on which to make a statement of what happened to them, and what steps to take.

*(*Manchester Evening News*, 2 January 1942)*

Part of a clothing ration book, showing coupons and directions for use. *(Philip Lloyd)*

She said, 'Well, I want to know before I eat it.'

So I said, 'Well it'll be gone, nobody'll notice!' [laughs] I said, 'well, I can always take it and flog it somewhere else!'

There was a lot of that went on at the Ritz, you'd go and sit upstairs in the balcony, and it went on like that.

NORMAN WILLIAMSON

There were some black market things, and I'm afraid it seemed to go on: my boss lived in Prestbury, and our drivers used to go into Prestbury, and quite often they'd come back with eggs, some currant cake which you couldn't get, things like that. The driver was picking up things, and we didn't do bad. And you could always get fish and chips! Always! So it was a bit of a standard diet.

DIANE SWIFT

On Saturday mornings my mother gave me a list to take to a shop in Walnut Street [Hulme] called Mrs Dore's: ¼lb lard, ¼ special margarine (*horrible*), four eggs, dried egg, ¼ rody [streaky] bacon. It came to about 9s [45p]. I paid the bill one week behind.

I used to go to Platt's toffee shop on the corner of Preston Street and Longworth Street, Hulme. He had a good variety.

The only thing I knew about the black market was in 1944. I was five. Father Christmas brought me a celluloid baby doll dressed in hand-knitted clothes: hardly any dolls knocking about in those days. I heard my mother tell the neighbour it was from the black market. My grandmother who lived at No. 128 Chester Road, Hulme, bought it for me. My father wouldn't do anything illegal.

I remember a house was empty, and there was coal in the cellar. But we couldn't take any. Looking back I don't think there was any black market in our street. There was no ready cash. We just struggled along quite happily.

ROY MATHER

My father had been a butcher; he knew plenty of butchers in the trade, he'd come out of the trade, but he used to come in with a tongue, no questions asked, like. You had to put this tongue in saltpetre to cure it, then my mother used to cook it hot and cut it up. So that was tongue sandwiches! [laughs]

My father kept a pub in Longsight, and they'd come in – 'Wanna buy this?' – you couldn't say too much, because walls had ears. They'd come in with cigarettes and other things. It was the Grove Inn, it's no longer there now.

The beer was frequent then, it didn't go short until 1946. In '46 we were closed two days a week, because the beer had run out. But in the war, you could get beer, it wasn't rationed, they never rationed beer. Like the bread, they never rationed that until 1946.

There were two chip shops near us, and you used to go and get fish, chips and peas, and they did beans in them days, you know like you get in Heinz beans? And then they'd shut up because the fat had run out. And then the other shop was open, the wire went round: 'Oh they're opening tonight!' – on the bush telegraph, you know.

T. MARRIOTT-MOORE

You have a look at the records for the butter or the margarine – what was it, two ounces a week? You had to spread it very carefully. My wife used to pull my daughter's leg: 'You've not got over the wartime habit of putting the butter on with a brush yet!'

Eggs, what were they, about two a week, something like that? Tea …

In the shops of course, a lot of things were under the counter. Now and again somebody would come up and say, 'Do you want any sugar?'

'How much?'

'Don't ask questions.'

A friend of mine was in charge of building a big airfield, and he was told that the workers, they got an extra sugar allowance. One day the local grocer called him in and said, 'Come here, I want to show you. I'm worried.' He took him into a little store room; there were sacks and sacks of sugar. He said, 'Your men have never claimed their sugar for six months. I'm worried.'

My friend said, 'Well, if you can continue to be worried until tonight, I'll relieve you of your worry.' He borrowed a big truck, and he loaded all the sugar and dispersed it. He did quite well out of it too.

There was this campaign to get you to keep bees, as a matter of fact. There was a special allocation of sugar for beekeepers, I remember. That's how I took up bee-keeping, because my wife said, 'Well surely they don't eat all that much sugar during the winter, and we could do with some of that to make jam with.' [laughs] So we took up beekeeping and had a little extra sugar for the jam making.

(North West Sound Archive)

No 'Condition'

In reply to Mr Molloy concerning oranges, I have an off-licence and general store and I am pleased to say I am open to sell to the public whether they come from Hong Kong or Timbuktu as long as they have their points book. I don't make any conditional sales such as most fruiterers do before you can get certain goods off them.

You can only sell them once so sell out of your window and remember, this war won't last forever.

E. E. Dennison, Salford 7

(Manchester Evening News *correspondence, 1 November 1943*)

SIX

YANKS

Even before the Japanese attack on US bases at Pearl Harbor in December 1941 precipitated the Americans into both Asian and European wars, there had been a feeling in Britain that the US were at least potential allies. The build-up of American troops in Britain began in January 1942, and reached a high-water mark in 1944 just prior

American GIs on parade in Albert Square in 1942. This was the first year of the American presence in the UK. A Division of the Lancashire Home Guard is in the background. *(Manchester Central Library Local Images Collection: M09823)*

to the D-Day landings. A total of around 1.5 million American servicemen were either stationed throughout Britain, or passed through on their way to the European battleground.

JUNE COWAN

The Americans were billeted in Withington and Didsbury in 1944. I remember drawing back my curtains one morning to see all these American soldiers standing at ease in two long rows along the grass in the centre of the road, together with all their kit, waiting to be taken to their 'new homes'. We had four billeted with us and they were all charming. They only slept in the house as they had their canteen nearby.

We learned later that they had arrived in Liverpool earlier that morning, having crossed over on the *Queen Mary*, then a troop ship.

In front of the Palatine cinema (where the DSS offices are now) the Americans had erected their kitchen and canteen facilities, which were always busy.

One enduring memory I have is of seeing a company of soldiers marching in formation down Wilmslow Road towards Fog Lane/Lapwing Lane traffic lights. They were all shouting in unison, 'Hup – two – three – four', followed by some words in rhyme, then back to 'Hup … ' etc. There were plenty of jeeps around, decorated with Betty Grable-type pin-ups and girls' names.

HOLD IT, BOYS — WE'RE SURE COMIN'

An *Evening News* cartoon from April 1941 illustrates the early expectation of a US–GB alliance. *(Manchester Evening News)*

BOB POTTS

My memories of the Yanks were up close and personal. There was a battalion based at Worsley Old Hall, officers and men, and during the Easter break in 1944 they took over our school playing fields, St Mark's School, Worsley, for their sports. Now, at the time we knew there were Yanks in the area because we used to see them in the village. They used to play baseball on our school field as well; they were like professionals, we went along just to see them play the baseball.

One day an officer turned up, a major, and he said, 'Do you have to use this footpath to get to school?'

It was just a rough old track, centuries old, and we all said, 'Yes!'

He said, 'I guess we'll have to do something about that.' And they built us a new footpath from Worsley Courthouse up to the old school. The school's gone, it's been rebuilt further away, but the footpath's still there.

The next American I saw, I was on the way from the orphanage [Ryecroft Church of England Children's Society Home] to school, during my dinner break, when three American soldiers approached me, and these were the first ones I'd seen apart from the officer, and they got near to me – they were in combat dress, they weren't in regular uniform, all tall, youngish, in their twenties – and one of them smiled at me and he said, 'We're gonna win the war for you.'

I thought, 'Oh, whoopee! Anything to get out of the home!'

A few weeks later they turned up in their hundreds for their sports on our school playing fields. They had a tug-o'-war game, and baseball, and a few other activities which I can't really remember. We were scrounging off them: chewing gum – they didn't give us any money – I don't think they could afford to give us any money! – but pencils, anything they had on them.

What struck me was that the officers and the men addressed each other by their Christian names. I thought that was highly unusual, but probably because they were all from the same town. The men were in their twenties I would say, and I think the major was about thirty; he looked like a movie star, very handsome. Although the men were boisterous, they weren't hooligans, but I noticed that the officers were watching them all the time. The officers never took their eyes off the men.

Also, they attended church, which was just a few hundred yards away from the school. So I saw the American officers at church.

BRIAN SEYMOUR

The only Americans I can remember was one Saturday morning when I was coming back from the butcher's; two American soldiers on Great Clowes Street, and one of them stopped me and said [in an American accent], 'Can you tell me where the Grozz-Veener Hotel is?'

And I said, 'Excuse me?'

'The Grozz-Veener Hotel?' And it was a pub, called the Grosvenor, and I've never forgotten that.

Manchester Racecourse was where the Americans had their base during the war. What was the racecourse, it's the university buildings now, Littleton Road [site of present Salford Sports Village, Lower Kersal]. During the war there was no racing, and the American Army took over.

American soldiers marching past Sale Town Hall during the 1944 'Salute the Soldier Week'.
(Trafford Archives)

DONALD READ

But what really brought the war home to us in Didsbury was the coming of American soldiers into our midst as part of the build-up for D-Day. They were billeted throughout the district, I think compulsorily. We had no room to spare over the shop, but Auntie Elsie had a box-room unused in her council house at Burnage, and my diary for 4 April 1944 recorded laconically: 'Auntie E has a Yank soldier'.

The Americans appeared quite suddenly in Didsbury village, walking around confidently in uniform or speeding through in jeeps. Most of them seemed to be officers, and I soon worked out the various badges of rank on their shoulders. I saw them at closest quarters in the village barber's shop, when I went there every few weeks for a basic 'short back and sides'. This was the British fashion of the time, presumably because it was a simple style requiring little attention, and so became the standard haircut for British soldiers. The Americans also wore their hair short, but with more styling. They expected to sit in the chair for much longer than we did, giving the barber detailed instructions about what to trim and not to trim. Obviously, they were used to dealing with full-blown hairdressers, and paying accordingly, rather than with traditional British barbers.

I never spoke to an American soldier, and my parents may also never have done so, for the Americans had no reason to come into our shoe shop. But I observed

US Band PLEA

Manchester is to celebrate the Anglo–American week. Is it possible for the American Army to provide one of their own regimental bands to play in Manchester and lead a parade of American troops through the city? They would receive a real Lancashire welcome.

S. T.

(Manchester Evening News *correspondence, 28 October 1943*)

them with approval, for I knew they had come to help us win the war. And yet, unlike those teenage girls slightly older than myself, who met Americans at dances and were given nylons (and babies), I was not excited by the American presence. I simply took it for granted in the circumstances. The American 'invasion' did not affect my everyday life.

(*From* A Manchester Boyhood)

ROY MATHER

There were Americans based at Belle Vue. Where the speedway was, and the Exhibition Hall, the government took that over, but prior to that the army was in.

American MPs at Piccadilly bus station, in the summer of 1942. (Manchester Evening News)

Then when the Americans come, they moved the army out and put their – they were coloured, it was a black unit. They were a transport unit, they parked all their vehicles on the car park at Belle Vue. Prior to D-Day, when they came, all around Burnage, round that area, they was billeted. These were white troops, they was billeted in houses, and General Patton was based at Knutsford – that was his headquarters.

All round Belle Vue, we used to go round, asking 'Any gum, chum?' That was a treat, getting the candy as they called it.

On VE-night all the Yanks were in town, and the Gaumont long bar was full of Yanks. The Gaumont long bar was on Oxford street, and it was by the cinema. They all used to come there, and all the girls as well.

DOREEN NEEDHAM

There is one thing I remember of that time. American soldiers must have had a barracks or something nearby, because they were often marching along Crossley Road in front of the school [Levenshulme High School for Girls], and as the railings around the school had already been taken away to go towards making munitions, it seemed like an open invitation for the soldiers to lie on the grass and watch us during our sports lessons – hockey and lacrosse. It's kind of sad to think about it now, as it's possible that many of those soldiers were killed on D-Day or thereafter. I wonder if many of them living remember Levenshulme?

(From the website www.levyboy.com)

MICKIE MITCHELL

I used to go to Burtonwood [US camp in Warrington]. I went out with one, he was a member of a Flying Fortress crew. Actually we were going to get married, and he failed to return. He came from Chicago, I would have been a gangster's moll, wouldn't I? [laughs]

We were out one day, four firewomen, and of course we were in uniform because you didn't get clothes during the war much, and we were in the Grand Hotel in Manchester. We were sat having a drink, the four of us, and there were these American officers sat at a table. My friend said, 'They keep looking at us, that lot.'

So I said, 'Yes, I've noticed.'

My friend said, 'We dare you to go and ask them to come and join us.'

So I said, 'OK.' So I went over and put my best voice on, I said, [in posh voice] 'Excuse me, my friends there would like to know, would you like to come and join us?'

So they said, 'Oh sure, madam.' So they came over, and that's how I met him. He was 6'4", and I'm 4'10"! [laughs]

But my mother wouldn't tolerate him. He used to come in a Jeep sometimes, with him being an officer, but she wouldn't let him in. I had to go out, 'Oh, he's here,' like that. Sometimes we didn't see one another for a long time, because I was on shift work, and he was off and back, like that. He failed to return from a raid.

I used to go to Burtonwood. Of course, their PX I think it was called, the equivalent to our NAAFI, it was dry, they didn't have drink or anything like that, so that's why the Americans sort of went mad I suppose, drinking.

When we were in Moss Side Fire Station, there were quite a few round there, and their military police were called 'snowdrops' – well we did, anyway! – because they wore white helmets. Ours were red, theirs were white.

BRYANT ANTHONY HILL

At that time I was in the junior school at Royal Oak [Wythenshawe], and it was a massive big playing field – they've got houses on now – and it used to run right down to the railway line. I used to wander down and watch the trains on the railway line; I was interested in trains before that. The railway line there, it was a short piece of about three miles between two big junctions: you got two lines at Northenden joined together, you got the short stretch, and it went into three lines at the other end [West Timperley]. There were dozens and dozens of trains going down; there were more goods trains in the war. This passenger train came down, which was unusual because there was none due at that time, and I stood there and it stopped: it was full of American soldiers, and they started throwing money out!

It was serious money. Now in them days, threepence or sixpence: you were lucky if you got that much. That was the first one, and we must have been the first children they'd seen. Coming through Liverpool, and they'd come up the dock lines and onto the main Cheshire lines, straight through to wherever they were going, and that must have been the first stop. I think the first time I must have picked up about two pounds.

We got one or two then, over a period of a couple of weeks, and we got told we had to take all the money in. Of course nobody did!

MARJORIE AINSWORTH

I remember the Americans being here. You often saw them, and a couple of the girls in the office had American boyfriends that they'd met at the Ritz.

One got pregnant. [laughs] There was a lot of that about. I remember another woman who was temporary with us having an American boyfriend, but she was married, and had to write a 'Dear John' letter to her husband abroad.

The Americans used to bring some amazing things over. They were very well cared for, they got loads of little specially printed novels and dictionaries and things like that which were issued to the American forces. They got rid of them or left them, they were great. Printed books were difficult to get.

You saw them in town, but I never had anything personally to do with them. I was married at the time, and my husband was over with the Americans in the Ardennes, he was caught up in the Battle of the Bulge. He was with an American radar unit, on a special mission.

DIANE SWIFT

I remember sitting on the doorstep in Hulme [Dunham Street], and the Yanks walking down our street on the odd occasion. We were told to say, 'Any gum, chum, please?' The Yanks I remember were kind people with a smile on their faces.

My dad was a long-distance lorry driver. He used to let me have the day off school sometimes, and always he would stop and give a Yank a lift. The Yank would always give me something: chewing gum or chocolate.

When I was about fourteen, my friend Irene and I would wander around exploring different places, which was daring in those days. I remember going to All Saints Park on Cavendish Street and Oxford Street. You could smell the rubber from Dunlop's on Cambridge Street, and we would always talk to a Yank and cadge a cigarette from him. He was very quiet and sad and just stared across the road. Looking back, he must have been homesick. He never said anything disrespectful and we met about four times a week for about six months. He often comes into my thoughts when I pass All Saints.

A girl I knew had a baby to a Yank; he married her, but she would not go back to America. She would go to the base in Burtonwood, and get £50 every month.

ANNIE GIBB

There were droves of Americans, down past the Palace, droves, along Oxford Road. I never went to that place in Warrington, there was a dance hall in Warrington [probably the Casino Club, on the corner of Bridge Street]. I didn't leave my own area, my dad was [shakes head disapprovingly]. Loads of girls used to go there dancing; they went on the train.

INSTRUCTIONS TO AMERICAN SERVICEMEN IN BRITAIN
- Don't be a show off.
- NEVER criticize the King or Queen.
- The British don't know how to make a good cup of coffee. You don't know how to make a good cup of tea. It's a fair swap.
- It is always impolite to criticize your hosts; it is militarily stupid to criticize your allies.

(From a US War Department leaflet)

JEANNE HERRING

I went out with an American soldier who came to the house. Mother made him most welcome, even though he was of Greek parentage. I wonder why her prejudice didn't work here. He bought me a pretty gold brooch. I had only known him for a week when he asked me to choose a brooch for his sister, so all unsuspecting I chose a gold one as he said he wanted a good one. When we got outside the shop he gave it to me. He was posted away soon afterwards.

FRANCIS HOGAN

The Americans were at what is now Trafford General [Hospital], they took over Davyhulme Park [Hospital] as it was in those days. They had it for quite a few years.

They used to come in the pub I used to drink in, the Bird I'th Hand in Flixton. They were very friendly actually. The landlord's daughter married one. He went and joined the Merchant Navy, he used to come into Manchester up the Ship Canal. She used to go down to the canal to see his ship, and he used to throw contraband to her! He got caught, and I think he got jailed for it.

A pal of mine, his uncle ran the Bird I'th Hand, and we were never short of a drink there. [laughs] The Yanks used to drink there. Not many of them, but quite a few.

They had a camp Warrington way, Risley [Burtonwood; Risley was the site of a Royal Ordnance Factory]. A lot of them used to go from there on the train into Manchester.

They used to get on well with the locals. They got on well with the girls all right! The ones I got in touch with at the hospital I got on OK with. In Manchester, they virtually kept themselves to themselves, except for the women, of course, they were all over them. They were a good crowd, young blokes like we were, out for a good time.

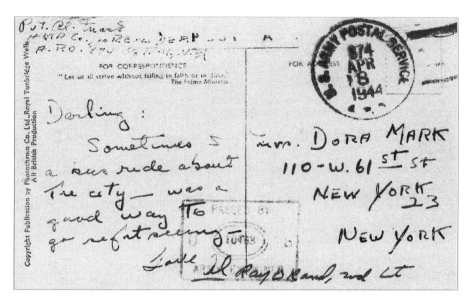

A postcard from Manchester, postmarked 18 April 1944, sent home by an American soldier to his wife in New York. *(Bob Potts)*

TREFOR JONES

No. 11 Chandos Road South [Chorlton-cum-Hardy] where I lived with my parents from 1940 to 1960, for twenty years. I used to sit on the top of this pinnacle [spherical gatepost top] here, and survey particularly the American soldiers. One lived at the Tomlins', at the house across the road, and there were several others billeted in the houses further down the road. They would come past, and I'd sit on the gatepost with the well-worn phrase, [laughs] 'Any gum, chum?' And they used to give you chewing gum, you know, the American chewing gum. And then they'd go on from here round the corner, turn left, and go to the old wooden St Werburgh's Hall, and that was the officers' meeting point, prior of course to the invasion. Why they were up in Manchester I've not a clue.

HILDA MASON

In the field at the back at Lostock they had a barrage balloon, and the Americans were there. The Americans used to go round, offering chocolates and things like that to the ladies, and I knew one or two that got pregnant through them. You know we were rationed, and of course nylons were very hard to get hold of because we'd only so many coupons to spend, but the Americans of course always had plenty of nylons and chocolate. So we were warned to keep away! [laughs]

I really took heed of what my mother told me, but there was a young lady round the corner from me who didn't, and I'm afraid to say her parents would have nothing to do with her; she was turned out on the street. I don't know what happened to her.

NANCY DRUMM

I remember the Americans quite well, really, because they used the park there in West Didsbury, a little recreation ground. On Cavendish Road, I think it was, opposite the school, and they trained there. And they used to walk down Burton Road singing, and they used to be whistling, every morning they did that. They were very sprightly and jolly.

They used to go to the dances, church dances as well to be honest, but also dance halls, like the Plaza and the Ritz, in town.

HELEN SEPHTON

We used to stop the Americans and say, 'Got any gum, chum?' [laughs]

We knew that they were American, you know, because of the uniform. You'd see the Jeeps going up and down, and you'd see them walking down Belle Vue way, mostly, down Hyde Road. Maybe they had a bit of free time, because Belle Vue then was the focal entertainment part of Manchester, really, wasn't it? It had a dance hall, it had the wrestling and boxing booths, it had everything – it had a zoo, it had a boating lake, but the main attraction would have been the dance hall. [Belle Vue Park was the base for the US Army 8th Air Force Service Command.]

ALICE CAMPBELL

Oh yes I remember them well, because two of my cousins – of course, we'd started drinking then – so we used to go to town, and the Americans would pour in, and they would just order and fill the table, and if you were around – which we were – they would say, 'You can have that, lads, because we're moving on.' And you never paid for anything. They bought it, and left it for anybody, you know. They were great. They were only lads like our lads, you know.

(North West Sound Archive)

SEVEN

COMING HOME

THYRA MATHER

There was a lot of noise going on outside in the street, and my mum went out to see what it was, and it was all these buses with very dishevelled soldiers. They were what they'd brought back from Dunkirk, and they brought them to the local baths [Cyprus Street, Stretford], so they could have a bath. And of course all the mums were out at the front, with tins of this and tins of that, and I think it was a tin of fruit that my mum gave this soldier, and he said, 'Just hang on a minute, hang on a minute, I want you to have something for your little girl.' And he felt in his pocket and out came this [shows a small gold crucifix]. It was black, it had gone all black, and he give it to my mum in her hands and he said, 'Now, you've got to look after this for this little girl, see that she always has it with her.'

The following are extracts from the POW escape story of my late father, Ellis Phythian Snr DCM (1919–1996), a private in the Cheshire Regiment. A resident of Bullock Street, Hulme, Manchester at the outbreak of the Second World War, he was wounded and taken prisoner when his platoon was cut off from the Dunkirk retreat in May 1940. His third escape attempt took place on 31 March 1943, this time from Stalag XXI-D (Fort Grolman) in Poznań, Poland, where he had been a POW since January 1942.

Private Ellis Phythian Snr, DCM, at the outbreak of war. (*Author's collection*)

I awoke after a fitful night at 6 a.m. to the early morning appel. It was cold and miserable. I looked through the window with its iron bars, and saw outside through the shaft of light shed through the window that it was raining: a mixture of sleet and rain falling into the moat which surrounded us. Despite the bitter cold outside my blanket, the thought of what lay ahead seemed to kindle a fire inside of me. I hurriedly dressed, and, leaving the room that housed myself and the twenty or so other inmates, I made my way to the place where my 'civilian' clothes were hidden.

When I look back over the years and think about those 'civvy' clothes I can't help smiling. The trousers were heavy-duty pyjamas dyed black; there was a khaki shirt also dyed black; and the jacket was an old sports coat I had begged off a Polish girl whilst out on a previous work party. It had obviously seen better days, and I had guarded it with the greatest care for many months. I completed my ensemble with a Polish-type cap, with ear flaps to prevent one getting frost bite in the ears. Donning this doubtful attire quickly, I then put my own uniform on top of it, placing the cap in my pocket.

[*As a member of a work party of POWs, Phythian was taken by tram to the worksite on the other side of Posen. His plan had been to hide in one of the trenches that had been dug for drains, but to his dismay he discovered that the trenches had been filled in.*]

On the worksite was a cabin where we had our meagre midday meal, and a long line of toilets. The latter were made of a light tongue and groove assembly, so I decided to get permission from the guard to use the toilet. Out of view, I would then kick out the rear side and thus get away. So I approached one of the four guards and asked if I could use the toilet. 'Yes,' he said, 'but be quick about it!' Thanking him, I made my way in. Once inside, I looked for a cubicle with rear boards that looked loose, and entered. Quickly I tore off my outer clothes revealing my 'civvy' gear. Through a crack in the woodwork I saw a group of Polish labourers approaching the toilets. I waited until they were almost up to me and then kicked out the back of the cubicle, striding out amongst them.

The situation would have been ideal if the Poles had stood their ground, as I could have mingled with them and got further away from our party, but unfortunately they panicked and scattered away from me, leaving me quite exposed, despite my trying to pull them back towards me. However, I managed to keep calm and walked on in the same direction in a quite unhurried way without looking back, nor to left or right.

It had become light now, and the sleet was beginning to fall again. After about three or four miles a sudden loud whip-like crack sounded in my ears, followed closely by another. I stopped in my tracks, heart pounding, expecting at any moment to be shot, but nothing came. My legs shaking, I walked on, and I was passed by a huge army truck lumbering along the road. As it passed, I noticed it was a diesel with fumes trailing behind. Realising I had been startled by a backfire, I laughed nervously to myself.

[*The original intention had been to rendezvous with a sergeant, who was to have maps, compass and a supply of non-perishable foods. However, the sergeant failed to turn up, so Phythian, having waited all day, decided to carry on alone. After receiving some slices of bread and margarine in a Polish woman's cottage, Phythian made his way to the nearby railway line. Here he spent the night hiding in some bushes, and eventually, as dawn broke, jumped onto the steps of a goods wagon of a slow-moving west-bound train and hid in the brake cabin.*]

After a while it was quite light and the train shunted into a sort of siding alongside some barrel-shaped wagons; perhaps they contained something like wine. Just as I was about to disembark and sample another train, this time a passenger train shunted onto the next line: it was full of German soldiers! It was not long before they got the same impression I had and tried to open one of the huge barrels. After a while one of them was successful and opened the large tap on the side of one barrel, filling his steel helmet with wine. I watched all this from my hiding place until, to my relief, my train made a sudden jolt forward and started to move. I was soon away from the soldiers and the wine.

[*The train reached Frankfurt-am-Main just as an air raid was taking place. Although the tracks were badly damaged, Phythian left the train and walked westwards until he was able to jump on board another west-bound goods train. He crossed the border into France just beyond Saarbrücken.*]

I had not eaten for days now, but the thirst was truly agony: I had to have water. As we shunted over the border into France I spotted a German policeman with a huge Alsatian dog inspecting each wagon on my train. As he came along the line, I managed to jump clear of the track to try and shake off my scent. I scrambled towards where I had spotted a shallow ditch and lay low while the policeman inspected the place I had just vacated! I saw the dog sniff the brake cabin and then look around to where I was hiding, but luckily the guard took no notice of this and pulled the dog's head back before proceeding along the line. To my relief he disappeared around the corner. It was then I noticed that the ditch I was lying in had water in it. Finding an empty wine bottle nearby I filled it with the doubtful looking greenish water and drank it through cracked lips. It tasted rather like urine, but I didn't mind as it supplied a service!

[*Phythian now continued his journey by goods train as far as Nancy. Here he left the train and followed the railway track on foot as far as the town of Toul, some 15 miles (24km) west of Nancy.*]

In Toul I again took a chance and knocked on a cottage door requesting food and water. A French woman answered and gave me a meal. She said she would bring someone who might be able to help me.

The 'someone' turned out to be the village priest. He was a large stout man, wearing the cloth of his profession, a black square hat and a long black cassock. He came slowly towards me with his right hand hidden under his cassock, his eyes penetrating and searching. I told him I was an English POW on the run, and gave him a brief résumé of my experiences, to which he listened with narrowing and widening eyes, mouth opening and closing with surprise (he spoke very good English).

After I had finished talking, I got the frightening feeling that this good priest did not believe my story. He brought his hand out from under the cassock and my heart leapt as I saw he held a small pistol. It was evident he had doubts about my genuineness. He warned me that if I proved to be an infiltrator, I would receive the business end of his weapon. However, I managed to convince him I was who I claimed, so he then proceeded to give me a map, a few hundred francs, some sausage and ration tickets for bread, then gave me instructions as to the route I must take.

He told me first to go to St Dizier, where I was to contact a one-legged barber (you may smile, but that was the God's honest truth!) who would direct me to Vitry-le François.

[*St Dizier is 50 miles (80km) west of Toul. The barber – who gave Phythian a welcome shave – gave directions to Vitry-le François, 18miles (29km) further on. Having walked from Toul, at Vitry-le-François, Phythian made contact with a Resistance cell.*]

I was approached by one Marcel Robert, one of the French Resistance group. He asked me for some means of identity so I produced my Stalag Disc 42450 and a letter from my niece I was carrying, the last one I had received in the POW camp. These satisfied him I was who I said I was.

The next day I was moved to a small empty newspaper shop on the side of the river Ornain. To get from the shop I had to cross a wooden bridge, as the original had been sabotaged, so it was guarded by a German soldier. I entered the shop with some trepidation as I was to be left there on my own for two days, dangerously close to the bridge guard.

Eventually Marcel came to me with a small pick-up type van which was loaded with long French loaves. To smuggle me past the guard he told me to get in the back of the van while he covered me with the bread and then a canvas cover. Then, my heart pounding, he took me right under the German's nose, over the bridge and away to near Châlons-sur-Marne, our next hideout.

At this house I had a clean-up and borrowed a pair of trousers. From there I was taken by Marcel Robert on to Paris.

I arrived in Paris in about the middle of May, and hid out with the Lebon family in Rue Denfert-Rochereau for ten to twelve weeks, during which time they were my only real contact with the outside world.

It was during this period of time that there was a purge on by the Germans which meant that I had to move temporarily from the Lebon household. I was taken by escort to a flat in the Rue des Bons Enfants. It was there that I experienced

An artist's impression, based on an old photograph, of the Rue des Bons Enfants in central Paris as it would have appeared during the Second World War. My father was hiding out in one of the upper storeys of the apartment block on the right when the hand grenade was thrown into the passing truckload of German soldiers. *(Phil Blinston)*

a most terrifying incident. A lorry loaded with Germans was passing by the block of flats where I was staying when suddenly someone threw a hand grenade from one of the windows into the lorry, wounding and killing some of the Germans. Immediately the flats were surrounded by the troops and an intensive search of the building for the culprits commenced. The two old ladies whose flat I was staying in had the presence of mind to roll up a small handkerchief, insert it into my mouth and wind a huge bandage around my face so I looked like I had mumps, hoping it would hide my poor French and not give me away.

I lay in the bed thus, shaking like a leaf waiting for the heavy knock on the door, when quite suddenly the noise of searching Germans subsided. Apparently the Gestapo had discovered that the missile had been thrown from the other side of the road. So it wasn't necessary for me to perform my masquerade, but it was still a nerve-wracking experience. The street was kept under close watch for a while after this incident.

At the end of twelve or so weeks back at the Lebons', the Resistance people informed me that I must be prepared now to carry on my journey as I had been there too long, and to stay there any longer would have been dangerous.

Quite openly I was taken to Bon Marché in the centre of Paris where they took a photograph of me. I was then given false identity cards and work permits which allowed me to work in various parts of France.

[*The Resistance also supplied Phythian with a rail ticket as far as Toulouse, from where he proceeded on foot to Tarbes. After short stays in Pau and Lourdes he crossed the Pyrenees, again on foot.*]

The huge challenge and mighty grandeur of the Pyrenees spread before me. It took us two and a half weeks to cross them, and that could be a tale on its own. I say 'us' as through the last part of my journey I had met up with other escapees, and now our small band had become ten in all. US airmen, RAF airmen, and a couple of characters who were silence itself: I never knew them to say a word to the rest of us all along the journey into Spain. Halfway across we were suddenly fired on by German planes patrolling the border but our luck held out.

We were interned in Spain, but eventually we were released when they discovered we were not armed. A Major Haslam, Military Attaché in Madrid, came to me. Shaking me by the hand, he congratulated me on having made it to a neutral country, and before long I was in the British Embassy in Madrid, where I was given a new suit of clothes and a decent meal. I was placed in the Hotel Mediodia awaiting transport to Gibraltar. I was, to say the least, on top of the world.

After arriving in Gibraltar in October 1943, I had another wait for a convoy leaving North Africa laden with troops after their African victory. I was to wait two weeks for the convoy but eventually we joined up with it and made a wide sweep into the Atlantic to avoid the U-boats, out around the Bay of Biscay, along the coast of Ireland up to Scotland and the Mull of Kintyre, straight up the Clyde into Glasgow and freedom!

[*Having returned to his regiment, Private Phythian was awarded the DCM by King George VI the following February.*]

BOB POTTS

My dad didn't come home on leave very often. I only saw him about six times during the entire war; mostly that was in 1944, when he suddenly turned up at the children's home in dress uniform – wow! He looked like an officer. I think the matron took a fancy to him, because she was single, and she was the same age as my dad. She made him a cup of tea and kept him all to herself for half an hour. He was a good-looking fellow, my dad, bit of a ladies' man.

HELEN SEPHTON

My father didn't come home until I was seven, because that's when the war ended. I didn't know him. There was this stranger walking through the door, I was absolutely in awe of him because I didn't know him. They talked about your dad, and he's fighting, and this that and the other, but you don't take it all in as a child. Then when he walked through the door, this stranger in this uniform, and he was tall, he was 6ft tall, and I was instantly afraid of him. And that stayed, because it was impounded by the fact that he was a very strict man. He never showed any emotion; he never put his arms round any of us or said anything gentle to us. It was all like he was still in the Marines, it was all 'stand up', 'sit down', 'come here', 'do that'.

This will mean giving up the job, going back home to four walls and washing up again. Or sharing the responsibility of the children, getting used to having a man coming in at regular times …

Even if you can do a clever thing or two with dried eggs, he is likely to expect something rather better.

Anyway you will have time to get used to the idea. They won't be demobilised as quickly as all that.

(Manchester Evening News, *8 May 1945*)

Now that the European war is over, isn't it time an official announcement was made reducing the period of overseas service for the army in the Far East to three years, thus bringing it into line with the RAF?

These men have done a marvellous job, and it is high time they received some recognition.

Mrs. R. Howarth, Delamere Road, Levenshulme

(Manchester Evening Chronicle *correspondence, 16 May 1945*)

DIANE SWIFT

I remember the neighbours saying two soldiers were coming home now the war had finished. They lived at No. 6 Dunham Street [Hulme]. One of them had lost his sight.

Hulme seemed to be alive with men in uniform: in the public houses, walking down Stretford Road, and getting married in uniforms.

Next door to my mother was a handsome man in the army. Next door to them was a man that served in the Royal Navy, and next door was a slight but good looking man in the Air Force. They called them the Brylcreem Boys for some reason.

A man called Percy who lived in our street came home from the Air Force (I think). He wasn't very well. He was very quiet, and looked sort of weak. Not long after he died aged twenty-nine. His mother and father never opened the front door for three weeks. I visit his grave in Southern Cemetery every Christmas.

FRANCIS HOGAN

I was demobbed in 1947. When I got back to Manchester, there were second-hand motorcars, everywhere you went; it was second-hand motorcars, here, there and everywhere. Ex-War Department ones: cars, motorcycles. You could get one for about twenty-five quid. I suppose that was dear, really, in those days.

I stayed at Metro Vicks for another three years, finished my apprenticeship, and went back in the Air Force.

DENNIS WOOD

I was demobbed from Somalia, or Somaliland as it was called then, in 1948.

When I got back to Manchester, everything was stood at a standstill, as it were. The superstructure of all the bombed sites had been left. They were just about beginning to pull them down and straighten them up. Mostly it was fire damage, you see, so it had burned them out and left a shell; the walls were still there, the roofs had gone. In some cases, where there'd been a high explosive which had blown then right down; the authorities had made an effort to flatten it out so you had bombsites. Hundreds of bombsites. It was like rubble, banged down flat.

Then the rationing of course was still on, I had another ration book!

BARRY ABRAHAMS

I didn't know who my father was, which sounds rather strange, because he went off to war, and one of the things that people don't realise is that when you went off to war you were often away for four to five years. And my father had seen me obviously when I was born, and then he went out to North Africa, and my first recollection of him was probably about 1946 – I'd be five. I was upstairs in bed, and there was a hullabaloo going on downstairs. That was my father returning home. Of course my mother was quite pleased to see him! So it was a relationship which had to start again.

It was difficult, but somebody who you had to get to know. You understood as best you could as a child, and then my brother came along, and we were a family again.

(North West Sound Archive)

EIGHT

CELEBRATING PEACE

Good news at last! *(Manchester Evening News)*

JEANNE HERRING

Ivan [boyfriend from Ireland, later husband] went home for Easter 1945. The following months saw the end of the war in Europe. I remember we both went into town for the celebrations. Great excitement everywhere, as we sat in a café on Oxford Road and watched through the window the hordes of people passing by, shouting, laughing and making their way into Albert Square.

ALICE CAMPBELL

They were going to have a party in Manchester, and I said, 'I can hear music, so I'll try and get to Albert Square,' and where Central Library is, in between the extension of the Town Hall, you were saying 'Excuse me, excuse me,' and you were stepping over couples. It was amazing. They were celebrating. Nine months hence there would probably be a lot of babies, but it was just accepted as the norm. I mean, you see pictures of how they're letting their hair down, and it was packed so jam-full, you couldn't get near any music.

And I came back, and I went to what they called The Cotton Club [Upper Brook Street], and they were celebrating there. And it was also – there were a lot of Austrians there, refugees, Jewish refugees, and I can remember I made myself sick on chocolate truffles made with cocoa, and they were delightful.

(North West Sound Archive)

ANON.

I remember the end of the war in Europe. We'd gone to bed and then there were bangs on a drum and everybody got up and the war was over. We went up to the town centre [Ramsbottom] and there was a shop where a man sold gramophone records and he played these records and people were dancing. Then we had street parties. The ladies made potato pies and they were allowed to use one of the chapels to make these. The best thing about it though, was that we didn't go to school.

(North West Sound Archive)

NANCY DRUMM

During VE Day I was in hospital. I was looking out of the window; all the staff had just heard about Belsen, and all the doctors were volunteering to go to Belsen and Germany. I remember that quite well.

MARY LLOYD

[Extracts from the diary of Mary Lloyd, Philip Lloyd's mother, May 1945]

Monday 7th May
Nice sunny day. Dried washing out well. Evening papers announced 'End of war in Europe'. Doenitz (Hitler's successor) ordered 'All Germans surrender'. The prime minister will not announce the end officially until tomorrow, but tomorrow, Tuesday, is to be VE Day and a whole holiday, and Wednesday as well, for everyone not on essential services. I got the washing finished and all ironed. It was after 11 p.m. before I had done.

Tuesday 8th May, VE Day
Shop open for papers and kept open until nearly dinner time. Very busy selling flags, etc., No staff in. Post Office shut. Put our big flag out. Started to pour with rain about 11 a.m. Cleared off about 3.30 p.m. Philip, Breta [daughter] and I went out on bikes to see the flags, etc. Another short shower. In for evening paper time. Then had tea in lounge. Opened a precious tin of peaches as celebration and had cream on it off the top of the milk. Then we all went to Manchester Road Church for the Thanksgiving Service at 7.30 p.m. Rev. Percy Bourne took service. Home again soon after 8.30.

Listened to Premier's official announcement of the end of hostilities in Europe at 3 p.m. We gave Breta a little silver bangle to remember VE Day, and Philip a pair of opera glasses.

At 9 p.m. we all listened to the broadcast by His Majesty King George VI. He spoke very well and clearly for about fourteen minutes. At about 10.15 p.m., we all went out to see the sights. Walked down Ryebank Road & through Warwick Road station and on to see Stretford Town Hall illuminated. It looked very well floodlit.

It was quite dark as we were coming back down Skerton Road and one building was floodlit red, white and blue. Lots of houses had fairy lights out. Quite a lot of bonfires going and plenty of fireworks about, including rockets. It was nearly 11.30 p.m. when we got in, Philip didn't get to sleep after midnight for the first time in his life.

The really official end of the war was one minute past midnight tonight, 8th May 1945. Hitler's Reich ceases its legal existence.

Wednesday 9th May, VE Day plus one day
Second day of celebrations and a holiday. Nice and sunny all day, much better day for weather than yesterday. No papers here morning or night. Some were printed but only a few so we cancelled those.

… Opened a jar of the apples I bottled last August and had custard with them.
… Wishart's [milliner's] had their windows a blaze of lights and had it set out in red, white and blue. Shop window lights are allowed these two days.

Thursday 10th May

Five years since Churchill became prime minister. Back to usual, school etc. today, and extra cleaning and clearing up after two days not doing much work. Children out of school 3 p.m. today and tomorrow. After the children had been in bed some time, Philip came running down to say that he had seen the specially illuminated tram passing in front of the shops going to Chorlton. He had heard a row outside and got out of bed to see what it was. This was about 9.15 p.m. Expected it would come back the same way then go down the Grove [Plymouth Grove] so called him again about 10.30 p.m. and woke Breta up to see it.

ANON.

It was a wonderful night, and when the actual peace was first declared, we went to Albert Square with my dad, and that was jam-packed with people. They were all happy, singing and dancing, and throwing fireworks up in the air, and everything. I'll never forget – it was euphoria.

(North West Sound Archive)

MARJORIE AINSWORTH

It was gas lighting of course, and I remember when it came on again, just before VE Day I think it was, we were in town, and the gas lighter was walking up Mosley Street lighting the lamps and he'd collected quite a little crowd of people who cheered every time a light came on. That was good.

DORIS WHITE

I remember it was the Tuesday the 8th May, and word got round that Albert Square was going to be the place to be that evening. Me, my mother and my cousin Hilda listened to Churchill's radio broadcast in the afternoon, and you got the feeling, you know, that there was some excitement in the air.

Hilda and I were in our ATS uniforms, and I remember we left the house and at the end of the road, by the bus stop, we could hear music and cheering

The crowds in Albert Square on VE Day, 8 May 1945. (Daily Mail/News Chronicle)

in the distance, down Stretford Road. Two full buses went past, full of people talking loudly and happily, singing and cheering. We got the third bus, also full of loudly celebrating people, and do you know the conductress wouldn't let us pay! [laughs] It must have been the uniforms!

The bus turned into Oxford Road, then pulled up about 100 yards further on. The conductress told the passengers that was as far as they were going, so everybody off and best of British! [laughs] We were still a good way from Albert Square, but nobody seemed to mind the extra walk. The crowds were already tremendous, walking in the road, so no traffic could have got through.

I remember we walked past the Tatler [cinema: also the Manchester News Theatre, and nowadays the Cornerhouse], which was showing a Donald Duck cartoon, I think, but nobody seemed to be bothered with that, there were no queues outside anyway. Hilda and I went round the side of the library, and by now the crush was so bad we had to struggle to stay with one another.

Eventually we made it to the base of one of the statues in Albert Square. There was a crowd on the steps but one of them, a soldier I seem to remember, pointed to us and shouted something like, 'Hey look, a couple of ATS girls – let 'em up here, lads!' So, slowly and with some difficulty, we squeezed through to climb two or three steps higher.

When I turned to look round at the square I was astonished by the massive crowd, and wondered how Hilda and I had managed to get through the area jam-packed with thousands and thousands of people. As far as the eye could see there was a crush of people, many of them in uniform, cheering, singing and waving Union Jacks, not only in Albert Square but also in the streets round about, as far as you could see.

The Town Hall had flags of all the Allied nations, and the singing was pretty well non-stop, 'White Cliffs of Dover', 'Run Rabbit Run', 'Roll Out the Barrel' and other popular songs being belted out impromptu from various places in the square, sometimes one song taking precedence, sometimes another. It was like a gigantic party, a huge celebration and letting-go after all the bad years. It was a couple of hours I'll never forget as long as I live.

It was such a fantastic feeling, we didn't even mind walking back home later!

BOB POTTS

I was transferred to a boys' home in Rochdale in 1945, and we had a lot of freedom there. The Master of the Home, Mr Bowker, said, 'We're taking you to watch the VJ Day celebrations near the Town Hall.' The VE Day celebrations had passed us by, we only got to hear about it from children at school. There were no radios or newspapers in the children's homes.

So there's a big park behind the Rochdale Town Hall, and the park is on high ground, and the Town Hall is on low ground, and so we had a grandstand view. There were fireworks going on; it could have been about 15,000 people down in the square, they were just going mad, you know. They were dancing, laughing and joking, shouting, dancing in the streets, singing, I've never seen anything like it in my life. It was jubilation. 'The bloody war's over at long last!'

DIANE SWIFT

We had a party. Tables were all down the middle of the street [Dunham Street, Hulme]. Buntings used to run across the streets and were displayed in people's parlour windows. I was only six years old when this happened, but I do remember the neighbours being very happy.

BRIAN SEYMOUR

We had a street party [Perkins Street, Salford]. We brought tables out and put them in the middle of the street, which were all cobbled. And there were flags hanging out of the windows, and they put bunting across the street. All the kids sat round, and we played games: blind man's buff. There were cakes and jellies and ice creams, and there was a corner shop further down, and she made home-made ice cream. What was she called? … Everson, Mrs Everson, and she provided a tub of ice cream.

MARJORIE AINSWORTH

We were expecting it, but I was working at the time in Openshaw, at the LNER; I was in the office there, so all the girls decided we'd celebrate by going to Belle Vue, which had a magnificent ballroom and always very good bands. So we went to Belle Vue ballroom, then I think we had a drink in the bar, and then one of the girls said, 'Come back to my place, I'll make some dried egg omelettes.' [laughs] I think we were allowed one egg a week or something, but you could occasion-ally get a tin of dried eggs which were all right for scrambling.

I remember dancing on that night and it was absolutely crowded, but I didn't go down into town.

FRANK ELSON

When the war ended … the headmaster at Deane Primary handed out the certificate signed by the king almost a year later and, going to my grandmother's house, all the houses had 'welcome home' banners outside, but that would have been well after the war finished, of course.

My most vivid memory of that period was being taken to the top of Quebec Street [Deane, West Bolton] at night to watch Bolton's street lights being turned on again. The time had been announced and there was quite a crowd. There were not as many houses blocking the view as there are today and it was quite spectacular. I was completely amazed. I had grown up in the dark and simply did not realise that street lighting was possible! I can't remember what I thought lamp posts were for, they were just there.

(From World War II: An Account of Local Stories*)*

T. MARRIOTT-MOORE

In Sale, I remember a parade, and of course all the organisations converged on Sale Town Hall with flaming torches, and I thought to myself, now this would make a wonderful picture, if someone were to shout, 'Hang the councillors up and burn the Town Hall!' [laughs] But of course the Town Hall had already been burnt. There was that, the torchlit procession, and there were various celebrations.

(North West Sound Archive)

ELIZABETH CHAPMAN

The country gave itself up to great rejoicing. What happened? What didn't happen! There were street parties, pub parties – every kind of party! Bunting and red, white and blue decorations were everywhere. Amongst other festivities, I was invited to a Victory party in a neighbour's house where again, despite rationing, cakes, jellies, sausage rolls, trifles, all sorts of goodies had been conjured up from goodness knows where, and there was great merry-making.

A little country pub called the Farmer's Arms, not far from my home, was surrounded by a picket fence. Every one of the struts had been painted red, white and blue. Union Jacks hung out of every window. People lit bonfires. Blackout curtains were taken down and thrown away forever. It was Double British Summer Time at that period so it stayed light until quite late, 10.30 p.m. or thereabouts. At their parties and bonfires people sang all the songs that had become popular during the war years: 'Bless 'Em All', 'When the Lights Come on Again', 'We're Going to Hang out the Washing on the Siegfried Line', and the never-failing and everlasting 'Roll Out the Barrel'! What a celebration!

(From One Child's War*)*

DR R.A. CRANNA

I was still a medical student on VE Day, and we had a grand time celebrating in Manchester in front of the town hall, standing on an air-raid shelter, dancing away. And on VJ Day, there were really very similar celebrations. I went back into Manchester where all my contemporaries were, and again we had a great celebration. I remember the next morning at the surgery the first patient in, he said, 'I don't feel so well, doctor. I think I'm going to be sick.'

I said, 'Excuse me,' and I went out and I think I was sick at the thought of it! That was the hangover.

(North West Sound Archive)

STUART CUNNINGHAM

I recall the night when a special train, all lit up with bulbs, came clanging down Manchester Road [to Denton] to announce Victory in Europe. It meant my dad would be coming home.

(From Denton Voices*)*

PHILIP LLOYD

On VJ Day a tram came past the shop, and they had the illuminated tram, bulbs all over the outside, and I remember my mother getting us up at about 10.30 p.m. to go to the front attic window to see this tram passing. I wasn't very impressed at the time!

HILDA MASON

We couldn't afford to go to Albert Square. In the streets and that, they put tables, and everybody made jelly, cakes, and whatever they could, and we had a real good celebration when it was all over.

And it was surprising how quick you got back to normal life, even though you'd had all those years of upheaval.

A modern-day photo of the War Memorial in Piccadilly Gardens, commemorating those killed during the Luftwaffe raids on the city of Manchester. *(Author's collection)*

CONTRIBUTORS

Names marked with a ★ indicate those interviewed by the author.

Harry Abraham
Barry Abrahams
Marjorie Ainsworth★
Bill Ashton
Roy S. Ashworth
Roy Bevan
John Burton
Alice Campbell
Harry Capper
Elizabeth Chapman
Joan Constable
Ivy Corrigan
Mary Corrigan
June Cowan★
Maurice Cowan
Dr R.A. Cranna
Stuart Cunningham
William Cunningham
Arthur Robert Davenport★
Nancy Drumm★
Annie Gibb★
Margaret Greaves★
Mary Malcolm Gregory
Frank Hargreaves★
Pat Hargreaves

Allen Hayes
Frances Henson
Jeanne Herring
Edward Higson
Bryant Anthony Hill★
Francis Hogan★
Dennis Humphries★
Jenny Johnson★
Trefor Jones★
Margaret Kierman
Marjorie Lloyd
Mary Lloyd
Philip Lloyd★
Ida McNally
Joe Marlor
T. Marriott-Moore
Hilda Mason★
Roy Mather★
Thyra Mather★
Nora Marjorie May
Mickie Mitchell★
Doreen Needham
Ruth Palmer
John Pearson
Harry Pexton

Ellis Phythian Snr.
Fred Plant
Bob Potts★
Olive Quayle
Donald Read
Ernest Rigby
Peter Roughan
Helen Sephton★
Brian Seymour★
Evelyn Seymour ★
Rosa Slater
Renee Smith

Ann Stansfield
Phyllis Stewart
Diane Swift★ [pseudonym]
Eileen Towers★
Hugh Varah
Doris Wade
Doris White★
Bob Wild
Stan Wilkinson
Dr Garfield Williams
Norman Williamson★
Dennis Wood★

BIBLIOGRAPHY AND SOURCES

Chapman, Elizabeth, *One Child's War: Memories of a Wartime Childhood in Stockport* (Metropolitan Borough of Stockport, 1990)

Cooper, Ian, Hardy, Clive, and Hochland, Henry, *Manchester at War: A Pictorial Account 1939–45* (MEN Special Edition) (Archive Productions Ltd, 1986)

Cronin, Jill, and Pilcher, Marion, *Denton Voices* (Chalford Oral History, 1998)

Gardiner, Juliet, *The Blitz: The British Under Attack* (HarperPress, 2010)

Hardy, Clive, *Manchester at War* (First Edition/MEN, 2005)

Hayes, Cliff (Ed.), *Our Blitz: Red Sky Over Manchester* (Kemsley Newspapers Ltd, 1945)

Howarth, Ken, *Manchester Wartime Memories* (Manchester Library and Information Services, 2006)

Hylton, Stuart, *Reporting the Blitz: News from the Home Front Communities* (The History Press, 2012)

Lavery, Brian, *The British Home Front Pocket-Book* (Conway, 2010)

Leach, Bernard, Hibberd, Helen, and Reed, Kate (compilers), 'Memories of Chorlton' (Manchester City Council, 2011)

Levine, Joshua, *Forgotten Voices of the Blitz and the Battle For Britain: A New History in the Words of the Men and Women on Both Sides* (Random House/Imperial War Museum, 2006)

Potts, Bob, *The Old Pubs of Hulme and Chorlton-on-Medlock* (Neil Richardson, 1983)

Read, Donald, *A Manchester Boyhood in the Thirties and Forties: Growing Up in War and Peace* (Edwin Mellor, 2003)

'Recollections: Heaton Park Memories' (North West Sound Archive)

'Recollections: Ramsbottom Memories' (North West Sound Archive)

Various, *Spirit of Manchester* (City News Supplement, 8 February, 1940)

Various, *Front Line 1940–41: The Official Story of the Civil Defence of Britain* (HM Stationery Office, 1942)

Various, *World War II: An Account of Local Stories* (Newsquest Media Group, 2004)

Wild, Bob, *The Dogs of War: A Prestwich Boyhood* (Bob Wild, 2008)

Wright, Simon, *Memories of the Salford Blitz: Christmas 1940* (Neil Richardson, 1987)

WEBSITES

www.nwsoundarchive.co.uk
www.movinghistory.ac.uk
www.britishpathe.com

www.chorltongoodneighbours.org
www.levyboy.com

For a striking visual record of Manchester's wartime years, especially of the Blitz, Messrs Howarth's and Hardy's books are highly recommended. Also well worth a look is the unforgettable ten-minute film 'Manchester Took It Too', produced by the film unit of the Co-Operative Wholesale Society, and available for domestic viewing from the North West Film Archive. Contact details (from April 2014):

North-West Film Archive
Archives+
Manchester Central Library
M2 5PD
Email: n.w.filmarchive@mmu.ac.uk

If you enjoyed this book, you may also be interested in ...

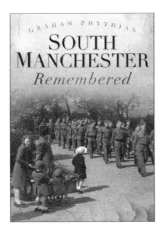

South Manchester Remembered
GRAHAM PHYTHIAN

Take a nostalgic journey into South Manchester's colourful past with this rich collection of tales from bygone days in the city and surrounding areas. Local author Graham Phythian presents a fascinating history, including sporting events (such as catching a greased pig), ghosts, murders, and even buried treasure!

978 0 7524 7002 3

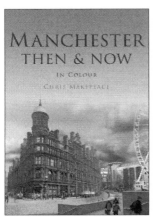

Manchester Then & Now
CHRIS MAKEPEACE

The city of Manchester has seen many changes – from the Industrial Revolution, through the destruction of the Second World War, and onwards to early twenty-first-century expansion and regeneration. Fascinating archive images paired with modern photography capture the changes that have taken place in Manchester in terms of its people, its society and its structure.

978 0 7524 6871 6

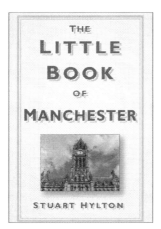

The Little Book of Manchester
STUART HYLTON

An intriguing, fast-paced, fact-packed compendium of places, people and events in the city, *The Little Book of Manchester* can be dipped into time and again. Here you can read about the important contributions the city made to the history of the nation, and meet some of the great men and women with which its history is littered.

978 0 7524 7947 7

Visit our website and discover thousands of other History Press books.

www.thehistorypress.co.uk